THE
BOOK
OF
JOB

THE
BOOK
OF
JOB

Translation, Introduction, and Notes
by RAYMOND P. SCHEINDLIN

W. W. Norton & Company   New York London

Chapters 3, 9–10, and 29–30 appeared originally, in different form, in
Arion, Third Series 4.3 (Winter 1997), 131–38.

The text of this book is composed in Mrs. Eaves
with the display set in Caslon Open Face.
Composition by Gina Webster
Manufacturing by Courier Companies, Inc.
Book design by Guenet Abraham

Library of Congress Cataloging-in-Publication Data

Bible. O.T. Job. English. Scheindlin. 1998.
The book of Job / translation, introduction, and notes by Raymond P.
Scheindlin.

p.   cm.
Includes bibliographical references and index.
ISBN 0-393-04626-5
I. Scheindlin, Raymond P. II. Title.
BS1413.S34   1998
223'.105209—dc21   97–37194
                          CIP
ISBN 0-393-31900-8 pbk
ISBN 978-0-393-31900-2

W. W. Norton & Company, Inc., 500 Fifth Avenue, New York, N.Y. 10110
www.wwnorton.com

W. W. Norton & Company Ltd., Castle House, 75/76 Wells Street, London W1T 3QT

Contents

To the memory of my father

Irving Scheindlin

1908–1991

Acknowledgments

A number of friends have contributed to this book by generously offering me their time and expertise. I particularly want to thank Katharine Washburn for encouraging me to translate a chapter of Job for inclusion in *World Poetry: An Anthology of Verse from Antiquity to Our Time*, edited by her and John Major and published by W. W. Norton in 1998; it was the experience of translating the one chapter that unleashed my previously latent desire to translate the entire book. Ms. Washburn also read and critiqued large parts of the manuscript at various stages, besides allowing me time-consuming access to her mental treasury of practical information about writing and publishing. Sharon Dolin, Lynne Sharon Schwartz, Lore Segal, and Michael Sells read portions of the manuscript at an early stage and helped me with just the right mix of praise and criticism. David Curzon gave the entire manuscript a painstaking critical reading from a poet's point of view and enlightened me on many points of rhythm and diction. Steven A. Geller not only read and reread successive drafts of the manuscript but put his vast knowledge of the Bible, Semitic philology, history of religions, and world literature, as well as his good taste, at my disposal at any time of the day or night. Robert Alter also read the translation with great care and made countless helpful suggestions. My wife, Janice Meyerson, contributed her critical acumen to the translation, her technical skills to the preparation of the manuscript, and her distinctive blend of wit and whimsy to the project as a whole. I was fortunate to have a careful and tasteful editor in Steven Forman.

The teacher who introduced me to the Hebrew text of Job was the historian Gerson D. Cohen, in a class he taught at Camp Ramah in the summer of 1958. His dynamic teaching and the dignity with which he bore the long illness of which he died in 1991 have been in my thoughts throughout the time that I worked on this book.

The translation is dedicated to the memory of my father. An immigrant to America at age thirteen, he introduced me to poetry when I was a small boy by reading to me the classic English poems he had studied as part of his completely successful struggle to master the language. He would often recite Psalm 100 (which he had memorized in the King James translation as a pronunciation exercise) and Ecclesiastes' poem beginning, "To every thing there is a season."

Introduction

Theology and Poetry in Job

Before there was a Book of Job, there was very likely a story of Job, an exemplary tale designed to teach a simple idea about religion and man's duty to God.[1] This story, which probably did not have a fixed text, is retold by the author of the present Book of Job as the narrative framework of his book. We may refer to this story as the tale of Job the Patient.

The basic story must have gone approximately as follows: Once there was a man of perfect piety, a man so pious that God, at the instigation of one of His courtier-angels, decided to put him to the test as He had tested Abraham. God afflicted this man with terrible suffering, taking away first his property and then his children and finally striking him with a painful, disgusting disease. At each stage, the man continued to praise and worship God. The man's wife advised him to discontinue his acts of piety and obedience to God, since they had proven worthless in warding off trouble and guaranteeing prosperity; his friends urged him likewise; but Job remained steadfast. In the end, God punished the friends for their bad counsel and rewarded Job for his loyalty, restoring his fortunes and replacing his children, so that he was better off in the end than at the beginning.

The moralistic tale of Job the Patient may be reflected in the prophecy of Ezekiel, written around 587 B.C., which speaks of three ancient legendary men—Noah, Danel, and Job—who were presumably already known to Ezekiel's audience of Judean exiles in Babylonia as models of piety.[2] Job's story was so useful to teachers of conventional religion that it survived the alterations wrought on it when the Book of Job came to be written, and it continued to be told and elaborated upon throughout the Middle Ages. It is reflected in Judaism in the Hellenistic *Testament of Job* and the midrash; in Christianity, in the New Testament and thereafter throughout the history of Christian preaching and art;[3] and in Islam, in the Quran and the Islamic stories of the Hebrew prophets.[4] It survives today in the stock expression "the patience of Job," referring to one who bears suffering without complaint.

At some point in the fifth or fourth century B.C., a gifted poet living in the Persian province of Judea turned the exemplary tale of Job the Patient into a literary and religious masterpiece by composing a conversation such as might have taken place between Job and his friends. In this new work, he imagined Job not as an artificial construct of the conventional religious mentality but as a real person tormented by God for no reason. Using the story as the dramatic setting for his poem, he converted Job the Patient into Everyman, and Job's suffering into an extreme case of what is endured by all who are subject to death and capable of reflecting upon it:

> Man born of woman:
> His days are few, his belly full of rage.
> He blooms and withers like a blossom,
> > flees, unlingering, like a shadow,
> > wears out like a rotten thing,
> > a cloth moth-eaten.

In drawing his protagonist as Everyman, this author ensured that the book would be read as a treatment of a universal theme unrelated to any political, historical, or theological issue peculiar to Judaism. He did this partly by identifying Job at the beginning of the book as a non-Israelite (probably as an Edomite, since Utz, Job's homeland, is connected elsewhere in the Bible with Edom, the desert territory to the southeast of the Dead Sea). He also makes the story's time frame purposely vague, for while most biblical narratives begin with some indication of when their events were supposed to have occurred,[5] the author of Job avoids locating his book in time. He also avoids any allusion to the people of Israel, its covenant with God, its Torah, or its history of kingdom (c. 1000–587 B.C.), exile (587 B.C.), and restoration (538 B.C.) to the land of Judea.

When referring to God, the author of Job strongly prefers names with pre-Israelite associations like El and Shaddai, or the neutral word *eloah* (which, when referring to the God of Israel, normally takes the plural form *elohim*); he reserves the proper name of the God of Israel, Yahweh, for the narrative parts of the book, never (with the one exception of 12:9) putting it into Job's mouth or the mouths of his friends. His quasi-pagan way of referring to God lends the speeches of Job and his friends a non-Israelite coloration noticeable to readers familiar with the style of biblical Hebrew. It is a feature of the book that I have been careful to preserve in the translation. The pagan tone is reinforced by frequent references to premonotheistic creation myths such as those known to us from Ugaritic and Babylonian literature. A non-Israelite, or at least a pre-Mosaic ambience, is also suggested in the first lines of the narrative through the description of Job's family's religious observances. These consisted of an annual feast accompanied by sacrifices offered by Job himself, as if the laws of the Torah did not apply to Job, or as if the Torah had not yet restricted sacrificial rites to the priesthood of Jerusalem.

All these devices create the impression that the story takes place in a vague prehistoric age, before monotheism was conceived,[6] before religious doctrine had taken shape, when people had no revelation or scripture to guide them but only experience and age-old received wisdom. The action of the Book of Job transpires outside Israel, outside urban society, and outside time. It is no accident that Shakespeare chose to place his most Job-like work, *King Lear,* in a vague, semimythic pre-Christian Britain—the Book of Job could well have provided him with the model of a laboratory for human suffering outside the realm of known time and established doctrine.

The author of Job makes certain that we will see the difference between the optimistic old tale that was his starting point and the far more complicated poem that he has built around it. He does so precisely by incorporating the former into the latter, so that the poem comments ironically upon the narrative.

In the narrative, Job is the traditional, patient figure; when his wife urges him to end his suffering by cursing God so that he will be struck dead, he rebukes her with an aphorism that summarizes the principle of religious passivity: "Should we accept the good from God and not accept the bad?" But only five verses later, Job launches into a raging speech, cursing the day he was born and demanding to know why he was put on earth if all he is meant to do is suffer (chap. 3). This curse generates the debate between Job and his friends. For twenty-four chapters of verse (chaps. 4–27), the friends and Job take turns debating the meaning of his situation.

The core of the book is this exchange of poem-speeches, which is organized in three cycles, with Job and the friends each speaking in turn. Eliphaz begins with a speech intended to be consolatory, but that opens up the question of the justice of Job's suffering (chaps. 4–5). Job replies irritably (chaps. 6–7). Then Bildad speaks, suggesting more clearly that Job himself is responsible for his suffering (chap. 8), and Job replies (chaps. 9–10) by strongly repudiating this accusation and raising the idea that he would like a hearing from God in which he might be vindicated. Then Zophar speaks (chap. 11) and Job replies (chaps. 12–14), ending the first round of speeches. The cycle is then repeated with speeches by Eliphaz (chap. 15) and Job (chaps. 16–17); by Bildad (chap. 18) and Job (chap. 19); and by Zophar (chap. 20) and Job (chap. 21), ending the second round. The opening of the third round follows the pattern. Eliphaz speaks (chap. 22) and Job replies (chaps. 23–24). Then Bildad speaks (chap. 25), but only briefly; Job replies, briefly at first (chap. 26), but then, in a speech that is introduced separately, at greater length (chap. 27). The cycle of speeches is followed by an interlude, the Meditation on Wisdom (chap. 28), Job's concluding remarks (chaps. 29–31), and four speeches by a bystander named Elihu (chaps. 32–37); these speeches conclude the consideration of Job's troubles by human intelligence.

At last, Yahweh intervenes with two speeches, silencing mere human discourse with His own sublime poetry (chaps. 38–42:6). His tone at first is sarcastic and angry; we are sure that His rage is directed against Job, for through the course of the entire poem Job has done everything *except* to bear his suffering patiently like his exemplary model. True, Job has not actually cursed God; but he has come close enough to doing so that we feel certain he is in for severe chastisement. Job has cursed the day he was born; he has demanded to know why man was put on earth at all; he has expatiated self-pityingly on his troubles; he has denied that he has committed any crime meriting extreme punishment; he has demanded that God explain His reasons for striking him; he has lamented that he lacks the power to compel God to submit to impartial arbitration. He has repudiated his three friends who attempted to console him with the kind of traditional wisdom of which the patient Job would probably have approved. And he has concluded by stating that nothing anyone will ever say will convince him that he deserves to suffer so. Thus, when Yahweh concludes His poem and the narrative resumes, we are amazed to learn that it is not the rebellious Job with whom Yahweh is really angry but the complacent friends! It is *they* who, Yahweh asserts, have not spoken truly, as has His "servant Job."

Many scholars see Yahweh's unexpected approval of Job and His anger at the friends as a serious structural flaw in the book. There is, indeed, a discrepancy between God's address to Job in His final speeches and His approval of Job in the narrative epilogue. Both of God's speeches are couched as a rebuke to Job: "Who dares speak darkly words with no sense?/ . . . Would you really annul my judgment,/make me out to be guilty, and put yourself in the right?" (38:2; 40:8). Both times, Job responds submissively, as if recanting his complaint (40:3–5; 42:1–6). Yet only a few verses further on, God praises Job and threatens to punish the friends.

This and other smaller discrepancies have distracted many critics from the author's essential unity of purpose and clouded their vision of what he intended to say. The poem cannot exist without the narrative, for the narrative's purpose is to establish the key fact against which the entire poem is to be read: that Job is right in maintaining steadfastly throughout the book that his suffering is unjust, and that his friends are wrong in maintaining that God is always just and that Job therefore must have sinned. The narrative enables the reader to witness the scene in heaven when the capricious decisions are made that destroy Job's every worldly good. We can therefore view the entire poem from Yahweh's perspective, a bold stroke on the part of the poet; with Him, we look down on Job and his friends and observe their pathetic attempts to make sense out of a life that we know need not make sense.

Like Yahweh, we know all along that Job is in the right and are willing to indulge him for a time in his puny human anger. When Yahweh appears at the end, He does not contradict anything Job has said, nor *can* He in our presence, because we readers know the truth as well as Yahweh Himself. Yahweh appears in the storm to confirm what Job has stated many times, that He and His management of the universe are beyond man's grasp and that He cannot be called to account. God's tone is angry not because Job is wrong, but because Job has not borne his suffering in silence, as had his model, the patient Job. But for Yahweh and the author of Job (no pietist, he!), this is a minor failing. Yahweh appears again in the resumed narrative to confirm Job's claim (and the reader's absolute knowledge) that he never deserved his suffering. The common point made by the concatenation of Yahweh's speeches and the concluding narrative is that Yahweh is outside human calculations of justice; man cannot know whether his suffering has any meaning at all, and it is impertinent of him to ask.

In the poem, Yahweh brushes aside Job's complaints and self-pity with a magnificent description of His own transcendent accomplishments. Job is not big enough to contend with Yahweh, and Yahweh refuses to contend with him. This is what Job has been saying all along. What other answer did we expect, when we know from the beginning that Yahweh is omnipotent and His treatment of Job completely arbitrary? Yet Yahweh is pleased with Job because, although he complained, he at least maintained the difficult truth that the author wants the reader to accept: that God's management of the universe is arbitrary, that Job was in the right when he asserted, "The good and the guilty He destroys alike" (9:22). He restores Job's fortunes because Job has maintained the truth. He threatens to punish the sanctimonious friends because they were willing to say anything, no matter how facile, pompous, or false, to explain away Job's suffering. We readers are glad to see them punished because we have watched them verbally tormenting Job, disassociating themselves from him in order to spare themselves the pain of facing the awful truth about life. Only if Job, whom they have injured, intercedes on their behalf will Yahweh forgive them.

Although the story doubtless had an earlier existence, it has been adapted perfectly by the poet to serve the sequence of ideas just described, and the match is perfect. By using the conventional tale as the frame for the poem, the poet satirizes its claim that we inhabit a world governed by justice and meaning. He demolishes the tale's innocent faith by means of his imaginary dialogue, which brings to the surface attitudes that the story was designed to suppress. He transforms the meaning of Yahweh's reward of Job from an acknowledgment of uncomplaining suffering to an acknowledgment that Job has grasped and intrepidly maintained the most terrifying reality.

We need not be shocked to find such pessimism in the Bible. Ecclesiastes, another late biblical book, similarly addresses the meaning of life and similarly rejects any certain meaning in man's activities or justice in God's management of the universe. If anything, Ecclesiastes is even more negative than the Book of Job: It presents human activities and accomplishments not merely as futile in the face of death but as a source of anxiety even at the moment they are being enjoyed:

> What comes to a man from all his labor and all
> the plans of his mind for which he labors under
> the sun? His days are all pain, his concerns are

all anger; he cannot even sleep at night. What
wind! (2:22–23)

In light of the dread fact that all living creatures die, there is
not even any ultimate advantage in human intelligence:

What happens to man and what happens to animals is all one. As the one dies, so does the
other; the same breath is in them all, and man
has no advantage over the animals. It is all just
wind. (3:19)

Nor is there any ultimate advantage in piety or justice:

All comes to all; the righteous and the wicked,
the pure and the impure, the man who sacrifices
and the man who does not sacrifice, the good
man and the sinner, the man who swears oaths
and the man who abstains from swearing oaths—
all have one outcome. (9:2)

Ecclesiastes is a different type of work from Job in its literary
technique, focus, and tone, but it resembles Job in its universal, non-Israelite character (despite having King Solomon as its pseudonymous author) and in its pessimistic
outlook. Speculations about the place of man in the universe and the moral implications of monotheism were clearly preoccupations of Hebrew writers in the late biblical
period, and we are fortunate indeed that the compilers of
the canon saw these books as suitable for inclusion in the

Bible alongside the books dealing with more purely Israelite themes.

So if the Book of Job is not alone in the Bible in its pessimistic, even nihilistic, message, we still must ask what positive message it was meant to bear; above all, we need to ask, why a poem? The author could have made his point in any number of ways, but he chose to write a dialogue consisting of poetic speeches, climaxing with Yahweh's poetic speech, and set in a narrative framework derived from an old exemplary tale. What did he intend to accomplish, beyond giving voice to pessimism?

To be sure, Job was not intended as a systematic treatise on the meaning of human suffering or on the nature of divine justice. Theology, an intellectual pursuit grounded in logic, did not yet exist. Even in the Greek-speaking world—geographically so close to Palestine, where Job was probably written—themes like those of the Book of Job were still addressed more through drama than by means of rigorous theoretical argument. Even the dialogues of Plato, though logically more rigorous than the Book of Job (with which they could conceivably be contemporaneous), retain a stylized dramatic form and often lapse into myth.

For Israelites of the fifth and fourth centuries B.C., existential problems were the province of teachers of "wisdom," the heirs of ancient Near Eastern traditions of proverbs, parables, and rhetoric. Such persons drew on a repertoire of material that crossed boundaries of language and religion. Wisdom in this specific sense comprised moral certainties, grounded in tradition and formulated in parables and maxims. When in doubt about what course to take or when troubled by life itself, even we moderns often reach for the appropriate maxim.

Ancient wisdom literature survives in Egyptian books attributed to Kings and couched as instructions for the princes, a form also known in Akkadian and Ugaritic literatures. Other wisdom-type adages, parables, and anecdotes have survived in collections in Sumerian, Akkadian, and Aramaic; in ancient Hebrew they are concentrated in Proverbs and occur frequently in Psalms and the prophetic writings. Ancient teachers of wisdom considered some of the questions that would later be raised by the Book of Job and produced books that may be its precursors. As early as 2000 B.C., a Sumerian writer told of a pious man who was struck with terrible losses and disease, but who was able to effect his own restoration through a fervent appeal to a god. Other ancient works having an affinity to Job include an Egyptian debate on suicide; the Egyptian "Tale of the Eloquent Peasant"; the Akkadian "I Will Praise the Lord of Wisdom"; and the "Babylonian Theodicy."[7] Not all of these works are as simplistic in their treatment of suffering as are Job's friends, but not one of them has the Book of Job's richness and complexity. The certainties of wisdom literature are cited in order to be refuted by Ecclesiastes and to be mocked to extinction by Job, but they are taken seriously in two nonbiblical works of the Hellenistic age, Ben Sira and the Wisdom of Solomon.[8]

There is comfort in wise sayings seemingly authenticated by universal familiarity and ancient tradition. Job, after being smitten by God, is a man badly in need of comfort. He appears to the reader not only as a man absolutely wronged by God but also as one for whom consoling speech-es on the meaning of life would be appropriate. Having lost his children, property, health, and social position, Job is a kind of mourner (mourning rites were observed not only by those who had lost a close relative but by persons struck by other kinds of disaster as well). His friends, appropriately, come to console him in his sorrow. They tactfully wait for him to speak first, though this means that they end up hav-ing to observe seven days of silence. When he has at last spo-ken, uttering his dreadful curse, they do exactly what their good breeding and inherited wisdom have taught them to do: They speak to him gently (at first) and tell him that what he is enduring is in harmony with the way the world was meant to operate. Their purpose is consolation, and their means is ancient wisdom.

For the exponents of ancient wisdom, consolation means assuring the sufferer that whatever disaster he has under-gone fits into a predictable universal pattern, predictable because it has occurred unfailingly in the past and has been formulated by the ancients in a proverb, parable, or poem. The friends also advise Job, as friends ought to do, how to extract himself from his troubles, or at least how to feel bet-ter about them, by relying on the same ancient wisdom. None of their behavior is strange to Job. He himself was a powerful man, a dignitary, presumably a man of good judg-ment, manners, and wisdom; he himself had had occasion to comfort mourners and sufferers before his disasters had struck, as both he and his friends find occasion to recall.

The problem is that ancient wisdom posited an exact cor-relation between behavior and outcome: A good person will succeed, and a wicked person will eventually fail. In consoling Job, the friends have no wisdom to fall back on but the conviction that he must have done something wrong. The first speaker, Eliphaz—obviously uncomfortable at saying so directly because of Job's well-established reputation for righteousness and because of the severity of his disasters— tries to get away with only hinting at this notion. But Job rejects Eliphaz's insinuations with anger and sarcasm. His responses bring about a hardening of the friends' position in the course of the dialogue, until, at last, Eliphaz, who originally had been so careful in addressing Job, accuses him of a whole string of specific crimes, of which, of course, Eliphaz has no knowledge whatever.

Job is certain that he has been righteous all along; and more important (for this is a literary work), we readers have absolute knowledge that he is in the right. We therefore sympathize with his repeated outbursts against the friends. We see even more clearly than Job himself the emptiness of the confidence they have placed in their simple rule of life. We squirm at the self-righteousness of the friends, who have not suffered and therefore assume that those who have have only themselves to blame. But the friends can only be offended by Job's refusal to listen patiently to their admonitions, which have been sanctified by tradition. How gratified they must be when God begins His great speech, toward the end of the book, by admonishing Job; how shocked when, in the narrative, God turns on them in rebuke and rewards Job for his stubbornness.

The Book of Job sets the terms for the discussion of suffering in such a way as to render meaningless the consolations of conventional piety, traditional wisdom, and theology. In their place, it offers a poem.

Job's narrative is dwarfed by the book's thirty-nine chapters of poetry. This poetry is so vigorous and engaging that it quickly turns the narrative framework into a mere formality, with the result that after Yahweh's great speeches we are almost surprised by its return. The chapters of poetry are organized as a dialogue,[9] but the book's point is made not by dialectic or by logical argument, as in Plato; it is made, rather, by poetic language and form and by rhetorical juxtaposition. As a work of consolation rather than theology, Job attempts to take control of our human agony, to give it full expression and tame it by means of imagery, rhythm, and wordplay. The poetry achieves this in two ways.

One is through sheer abundance, for simply as a collection of poems, Job is a remarkable achievement. If we disregard who is speaking and the purpose or context of his remarks in the structure of the book, we can easily isolate segments from the speeches to create an anthology of short poems on a variety of situations and moods. Take Eliphaz's night vision (4:12–16); Job's hymns (9:4–10; 26:1–14) and his anti-hymn (12:9–25); Job's anger (chap. 3); self-pity (7:3–6); and self-loathing (9:30–31). The book is replete with poetic observations of nature and social life—quick vignettes, sometimes realistic, always lively and colorful. Some of these, being tangential to the argument in which they occur, give the impression of being little poetic set pieces that may have had an independent existence and were incorporated by the author into the book from other works.[10] Examples are the description of a dry riverbed

(6:15–20); a papyrus plant (8:11–12); a tangled weed (8:16–18); a tree stump (14:7–9); a warrior (15:26); a rich man's household, with wife, children, servants, and visitors (19:13–19); the treatment of peasants by the rural rich (24:2–11); and the activities of urban criminals of the night (24:12–17). Particularly notable are the extended reminiscences of Job as the chief householder of a city, all-powerful dispenser of charity and justice, both feared and admired (chap. 29); and the complementary description of his social position in his decline, spurned by men born below his status, attacked by outlaws and riffraff (30:1–10). And all this before we arrive at Elihu's lengthy description of a storm (36:27–37:22) and the two great nature poems that make up Yahweh's speech from the storm (chaps. 38–41).

All of this poetry was not written merely to decorate the book. Its energy and exuberance, palpable from the very beginning and hardly ever fading during the work's long course, keep present before us the fact that we are reading the work of a writer who is fascinated with this life, troubled as it is, a man who never wearies of the variety and vividness of the multitude of things that life offers for our observation. In this, he is the temperamental opposite of the world-weary Ecclesiastes, who suffers from surfeit as Job suffers from deprivation. Ecclesiastes finds all things wearying, repeating themselves in an endless round of life and death in which nothing really new ever happens; he finds life's abundance, which is so invigorating to the author of Job, to be as insubstantial as a vapor. To the author of Job, the world pulsates with life. He expresses everything with vehemence; he is passionate about injustice, and about everyday life in its glorious detail. Even while raging at God's tyranny, he cannot help but hymn, in a passage of melting beauty, the mystery of his own conception and birth. He may rage at injustice, and he is at least as conscious of death as Ecclesiastes, but never in his forty-two chapters does he ever come close to saying, "Vanity of vanities, all is vanity."

Job's poetry achieves the book's purpose of consolation partly by providing its own vigor as an antidote to its pessimism, by changing the level of the discussion from a meditation on life's injustice to a parade of life's sheer multitudinousness. The poetry is in part a vehicle for steering us away from the suffering with which life burdens us toward the delight at what life has to offer. This is not a quantitative argument. The author does not make the simplistic claim that life's delights are commensurable with or compensation for life's sorrows. He does not make any argument at all. All arguments have been rendered nil by the book's premise. Since the narrative presents Job's complaint as rational and correct, there is no room left for a rational solution. Rather, poetry is used to shift the ground from reason, where life must lose, to emotion, where it at least has a chance.

The other way in which the poetry functions is to give full expression to Job's, and therefore our own, grief and anger. Expressions of grief abound in the Bible: We think of David's lament for Absalom; of Jacob's for the presumed-dead Benjamin; of the psalmist for various kinds of suffering and loss; of the poet of Lamentations for the destroyed Jerusalem. But Job is the one biblical character who voices the anger associated with suffering and bereavement. His anger arises from his own demand for meaning, from a refusal to yield emotionally to the terrible pointlessness of our suffering. Job is never reconciled; his heart demands meaning, even though intellectually he intuits (and we know) that he cannot have it. He is constitutionally incapable of falling into Ecclesiastes' sybaritic languor, which to him would be a kind of effete submission. Job knows and hates the truth, hates it precisely because he remains engaged in life. The paradoxical meeting of the book's pessimistic assumptions and this vigorous engagement in life is what produces its anger and its poetry. That is why it is a more profound literary creation than Ecclesiastes, whose tone and message are more simply interrelated.

Job's anger helps tame ours and bring it into manageable compass; this itself is a kind of consolation. We read Job not because it provides answers to our questions, consolation for our grief, or redress for our anger, but because it expresses our questions, grief, and anger with such force.

Poetic Form

Biblical Hebrew poetry is not grounded in a strict meter like traditional English syllabic-accentual verse or Latin quantitative meter. Its rhythm derives more from the balancing of images and ideas than from the strict patterning of words or accents. It has a loose meter in which certain patterns of word stress are used to reinforce the dominant poetic device, which is syntactic-semantic parallelism. Its basic unit is a verse that is subdivided syntactically, usually into two clear parts (the technical term is "hemistichs," but here I use the term "lines"). These verses, the units that are traditionally numbered for easy reference, may contain one or two sentences, or they may consist of incomplete clauses or phrases linked with the preceding or following verses. The two lines that constitute the verse normally consist of statements of approximately equal length that are semantically or syntactically balanced against each other and that sometimes are nearly identical in meaning. An extreme example is:

> one breath from God and they perish;
> one snort from Him and they're gone. (4:9)

These two lines have the same grammatical structure, the same length (three Hebrew words each), and the same number of stresses (three each); they employ similar images to make the same point, and they are virtually synonymous.

Very few lines of biblical verse are as strictly correlated as this pair. The ways in which two lines can complement each other are myriad, though some degree of synonymity is usually present. The reader's pleasure comes from experiencing the ever-shifting semantic relationships between the pairs of lines as they succeed each other, and from the concision of expression enforced by the parallelism.

Hebrew verse may also be written in three-line groups, but only rarely do all three lines share the parallelism; in such cases, the first line may be a kind of heading, followed by a parallel couplet that amplifies, contrasts with, or responds to it:

> Black take that night!
> > May it not count in the days of the year,
> > may it not come in the round of the months.
> > (3:6)

Biblical parallel verse is a flexible instrument capable of an infinite number of effects, yet with all its possible variations, the form itself always remains recognizable. A good anthology of types of parallelism may be found in 28:20–26.

The poetry in Job is also distinguished from the prose by its use of language. The book begins and ends in textbook Hebrew prose resembling the narratives of the patriarchs in the Torah for clarity and simplicity, while the poem that occupies the bulk of the book uses the elevated diction characteristic of Psalms and the prophets, emphasized by the constant parallelism. But the poem itself is not uniform in style. For long stretches, such as Job's curse (chap. 3), it is clear and elegant, making merely the kinds of demands on the reader's imagination made by poetry in general, especially by poetry packed with imagery. But other parts of the poem are obscure.

A striking feature of the Book of Job's style is the richness of its vocabulary. We can see the author indulging himself in it when he deploys five words for "lion" in a passage describing starving lions (4:10–11); the reader of this translation may be surprised to discover that English has only one word for the king of the beasts. Similarly, in describing the value of wisdom, he heaps up four different words for gold (28:15–17); again, English has only one. Job's author also has many words for trapping, which he is happy to concentrate in Bildad's description of the fate in store for the wicked man (18:8–11); the passage uses no fewer than six words for traps, snares, and ropes, and perhaps some verbs that we no longer recognize as technical terms in the craft of trapping, for the passage is not completely intelligible. The difficult verses on the impossibility of catching the aquatic monster here called the River Coiler contain several known technical terms from the craft of fishing, but much of this passage is obscure, probably because buried in it are other such terms no longer known to us. When several obscure words occur together in a single verse, or when an obscure word occurs within an image that itself is unclear, the context may not provide enough clues to yield clarity, and scholars may disagree on what meaning to assign a word, a verse, or even a whole passage.

Many of the difficulties in the Book of Job may be so because the meanings of many words were forgotten when Hebrew ceased to be a spoken language in the first or second century A.D. Words now rare may have been common at the time of the author; perhaps they were even colloquial words that by accident are found only in the Book of Job, but in contexts too obscure for us to guess at their meaning. There are more words in Job that occur only once in the Bible than in any other biblical book.

Job also contains many grammatical and syntactic anomalies: use of the singular where we would expect the plural, and vice versa; of the feminine where we would expect the masculine, and vice versa; unusual pronominal suffixes; and other peculiarities. But these peculiarities do not occur regularly enough to permit us to speak of Job as being written in a special dialect. Many passages contain only familiar words, or at least familiar roots, and present few grammatical difficulties, but still do not yield a meaning on which all readers can agree. Job contains more obscure words, phrases, and passages of disputed meaning than any other book of the Bible. Among Hebraists, it is a notoriously difficult book.

Some of the difficulties in Job are probably the result of textual errors that occurred as the book was copied over the centuries. It is widely agreed that the text of the Bible is full of errors, and much scholarly energy has gone into attempting to divine the correct original text. (This procedure will be discussed in more detail later.) The principle is certainly correct, for it is reasonable to suppose that a book transmitted over such a long period would have suffered some injury. But this supposition is not adequate to explain the peculiarly difficult language of the Book of Job. For one thing, it is not clear why Job would have been more subject to corruption than other biblical books. For another, we must bear in mind that the period in which the book must have suffered all these corruptions is not the entire period from the time it was composed until now, but only the 300 to 400 years between its composition and the earliest extant witnesses to the text, which, though fragmentary and abridged, are not radically different from the standard consonantal text. Though the text has certainly suffered some corruption, I doubt that problems of transmission are a sufficient explanation for the book's special difficulties.

More plausible is the belief of some scholars that the Book of Job was couched by the author in difficult language in order to obscure his unorthodox ideas. This approach at least attributes the book's diction to authorial intent, but it is still an extrinsic approach because it implies that the style is merely a mask, the use of which was dictated by an outside force, such as the opinions of the public or of religious authority. Yet there is no reason to suppose that opinion on the themes of Job was so entrenched in the author's day as to render dangerous or even unpopular his giving voice to them in a book; Ecclesiastes shows that such matters were written about openly. We must not read back into the late biblical period the medieval and early modern notion that Judaism has always had one specific set of officially approved doctrines. Furthermore, not all of the ideas that could be considered nonorthodox in Job are written obscurely. Some of Job's harshest accusations against God are written in lucid basic Hebrew, intelligible to this day to any Hebrew-speaking schoolchild.

Job's difficult language is part and parcel of the poem. Many poetic traditions favor a difficult style simply as a convention of poetic diction. This tendency is documented in some Babylonian wisdom writings.[11] It is not foreign to the Bible (Isaiah and Hosea contain long sections of difficult poetry) and even became a hallmark of Hebrew poetry in the early Middle Ages. Obscurity of language can have a mimetic function: Confusion of language can be used to imitate confusion of ideas, to depict a speaker as being momentarily at a loss, or to represent the breakdown of intellectual control in the vehemence of debate. But beyond all local mimetic explanations, the author of Job may have decided that a difficult texture was the right one for his emotionally wrenching theme—a tortured language to describe life's torment.

Difficult passages are not necessarily hermetic. When one who knows Hebrew well reads Job as a poem, stretches of difficult text are illuminated by flashes of intelligibility that combine with texture to create a definite tone and mood within a general framework of meaning. The result is evocative and suggestive, because individual words have meaning even if their connection is obscure, and because nearly every Hebrew word has an identifiable root that gives the reader glimpses of meaning even when he cannot see exactly what is meant. Such passages imitate the way our own minds work in grappling with Job's eternal theme, now granting us flashes of meaning, now throwing obscurity over all. Intelligible or not, the Book of Job's difficult language is an appropriate vehicle for its subject.

The Shape of the Book

The regularity of the three cycles of speeches is matched by the regularity of the construction of the individual speeches. Most of the speeches of the friends, Job's replies to these speeches, and the speeches of Elihu are constructed according to a three-part plan: They begin with a verse or more in which the speaker addresses his auditors or refers to something just said, after which follows the bulk of the speech and sometimes a peroration. But just as the plan of the three cycles of speeches is not carried through to completion, so the plan of the individual speeches is not carried through with any rigor, and some of the speeches include only one or two of these sections.

The apparent regularity of form inevitably suggests to the

first-time reader that there will be a clear progression of ideas from speech to speech. Yet no such progression can be convincingly charted. Sometimes a speech opens by referring directly to the preceding speech, but then veers in a different direction. Often a speaker seems to echo and satirize the words of a preceding speaker, but not necessarily those of the speaker immediately preceding. Many of the speeches are so loosely written or lapse into such obscure language that it is not possible to write a précis that accounts for every verse. In the notes, I have provided summaries of the speeches to help guide the reader through each speaker's train of thought, but I have no desire to impose a strictly logical progression where no amount of previous scholarship has been able to demonstrate the existence of one.

Yet some broad patterns can be discerned. There is a general, though not consistent, intensification of the friends' accusations of Job over the three cycles. In the first round, Eliphaz is rather encouraging and assures Job that better times will come for him; Bildad hypothesizes that Job's sons may have sinned, and suggests that if Job supplicates God he will doubtless obtain relief; Zophar says that if Job will examine his own ways he will realize that he has committed crimes and that God is punishing him less than he deserves, but that if he makes restitution and supplicates God he can yet be restored. Up to this point, no one has stated baldly that Job has definitely sinned. In the second round, Eliphaz mocks Job, saying that his own words reveal his guilt; he goes on to describe the doom awaiting the sinner, implying that this is the doom awaiting Job but without saying so explicitly; Bildad and Zophar dilate on this theme without referring

to Job at all. In the third round, Eliphaz finally bursts forth
with the wild accusation, "Your evil is tremendous, your sins
unending" (22:5). In this, the last full-length speech by one
of the friends, Eliphaz subjects Job to a series of specific and
completely imaginary accusations, which he states as plain
fact. Though mitigated by Eliphaz's vision of the restoration
that Job can achieve by "returning" to God (22:23, the only
occurrence in the book of the Hebrew term for repentance),
the speech seems to be the climactic indictment. After it
comes only Bildad's short speech, which begins with a hymn
to God's greatness and, until it is abruptly broken off, seems
to be modulating to the theme of the sinfulness of man in
general in God's eyes, as if intending to cool the tone by
shifting the focus away from Job. Zophar's third speech is
either missing, subsumed into Job's second reply to Bildad,
or was never written.

Job's speeches in reply to the friends also show some progression, though not a consistent one. In the first round,
his reply to Eliphaz, after a long introduction, continues the
theme of his curse, expatiating on his misery and wish for
death; but it also generalizes from Job's personal fate to the
fate of man in general, and toward the end it raises the question of why God cares so much about man's behavior, showing that Job has gotten Eliphaz's hint about his having
sinned. In his reply to Bildad, one of the book's highlights,
Job attacks God directly as a tyrant, and raises for the first
time the thought of a confrontation with Him. In reply to
Zophar, Job elaborates on the fantasy of a confrontation
with God, now addressing Him directly in an ironic sum-
mons that he admits will never be answered. Knowing that

he can never achieve vindication in this way, Job fantasizes briefly about being hidden away in the grave until God's anger passes, so that they can then be reconciled; but he dismisses this vision, knowing that there is no afterlife.

Job's reply to Eliphaz in the second round dilates on God's merciless attack and the extent of his suffering; he even associates the friends with God as being the cause of his suffering. His reply to Bildad replaces his idea of vindication after death with the fantasy of a kinsman who might someday come forward to avenge him. In his reply to Zophar, he asserts for the first time that not only do the righteous, like himself, suffer, but the wicked actually prosper. It would seem to be this statement that triggers Eliphaz's aggressive speech that opens the third round, in which he accuses Job of specific crimes. But Eliphaz's speech does not divert Job from this theme, for he replies with an elaborate description of the extent of evil tolerated by God in the world.

In Job's reply to the little hymn that constitutes Bildad's truncated third speech, he seems to turn on Bildad in a fury, as if saying that he does not need instruction from him about God's power and can speak just as eloquently on the subject himself. After this outburst, Zophar does not dare speak up. Instead, there is another speech by Job, in two parts. In the first, he definitively denies that he has done anything wrong. In the second, he curses his enemies, demanding that all the punishment that the friends have claimed is the lot of the wicked should befall his own enemies; it seems plain that the enemies he is cursing are the friends themselves, just as it was clear in the earlier chapters that when the friends spoke of the doom of the wicked, they were referring to Job. In issuing this curse, Job employs the same moralistic terms that the friends had employed against him, as if to say: If you are right that only the wicked suffer, I pray that those who have wronged me suffer the torments that you claim are their lot. In this way, everything Job says that echoes the opinion of the three friends should be understood as ironic.

This summary of the three cycles of speeches by Job and the friends shows that while the speeches do not constitute a dialogue of systematically defined ideas organized in a clear progression, neither are they static. There is a loose organization. At the same time, the speeches are notable more for their expression than for their logical development. This is exactly what we would expect of a book that wrestles with ultimate existential problems in language inherited from ancient Near Eastern literary traditions, a book written before the Near East was swept by Hellenistic patterns of abstraction and logic; at the time the Book of Job was composed, these patterns of thought were just in the process of emerging in Hellas itself.

Even after the cycle of speeches has ended, Job still has much to say. But before his final speeches comes the Meditation on Wisdom (chap. 28), the only poetry in the book that is not attributed to any particular speaker. The contents of the Meditation on Wisdom are closely related to the message of the book as a whole. This message, artfully prepared for by the chapter's first twenty-seven verses, is the statement in the chapter's last verse (28:28) that the world *is* managed by divine wisdom, but that that wisdom is beyond man's apprehension; man's only recourse, therefore, is piety and silence. Thus, the Meditation on Wisdom can be seen as preparation for the divine speeches at the end of the book, spelling out the message not stated explicitly in the speeches themselves. Most scholars agree that this poem is not part of the original book, since it interrupts the dialogue and, by anticipating Yahweh's message, renders His speech anticlimactic. These particular objections, however, are not very weighty, for, as we shall see, the book is full of repetitions and anticipations, being constructed by concatenation rather than by the requirements of drama. And the Meditation is certainly functional in terms of the book's overall plan, for it provides a needed change in tone from the vehemence of Job's speech in chapter 27 to a cool solemnity, a contrasting background for Job's impassioned concluding soliloquies.

If there is any purely literary objection to the Meditation on Wisdom, it is not that it renders the end of the book anticlimactic, but rather that it bluntly states a concrete message, while the author of Job has struggled for forty-two chapters to replace all messages with poetry, a much harder and more sophisticated project. The literary form of the Meditation derives from the certainties of wisdom literature, while the rest of the book is grounded in the ambiguity and conflict characteristic of real poetry. For all its graceful writing and excellence of form, the Meditation on Wisdom is simply too straightforward to match the subtlety of the book as a whole. On an emotional level, the Meditation on Wisdom seems to derive pious satisfaction from the distance between the mind of God and the mind of man; it reflects none of the anxiety that this distance causes Job in the rest of the work. Yahweh's two speeches may boil down to the same abstract idea as the one expounded in the Meditation on Wisdom, but in emotional pitch these passages are completely different. Wisdom preaches; Yahweh crushes.

After the Olympian view of the universe couched in the oracular voice of the Meditation on Wisdom, we experience the return to Job, the suffering individual who speaks in chapters 29 and 30, as a powerful poetic reproach to all theoretical doctrine. In these chapters, Job speaks at length of his social downfall, contrasting his former status as a respected authority in his community with his present status as an object of derision. In chapter 31, he protests his innocence one last time in a lengthy oath that closes his case.

The speeches of Elihu are viewed by many as presenting a structural problem similar to that of the Meditation on Wisdom. From a purely dramatic point of view, it might have been best if Yahweh's speeches had followed immediately upon Job's concluding oath; and a reader who demands an absolutely rational sequence of ideas may feel that Elihu's speech describing the storm renders Yahweh's speech that immediately follows anticlimactic. But we would not dispense with Elihu for all the world. Not only do his speeches contain some of the book's best poetry; they also create a character who is a real personality rather than a name attached to a speech. Of all the speakers in the book, including Job, Elihu is the one whose character is most distinctly realized, through speeches that project the almost comical personality of a brash and crudely self-assured young man. His opening speech is prolix and repetitive, as if, thrilled to have the floor at last, he cannot stop his flow of words or control his desire to shine. Both the narrator and he himself stress that he is junior to the others, perhaps to imply that he is merely a younger, more impulsive version of the grave Eliphaz, Bildad, and Zophar. In his inexperience, he reveals the weakness of character and intellect that is partly masked by the more polished speech of his seniors. But his gift for rhetoric comes out plainly in the description of the storm in his fourth speech, one of the poetic highlights of the book. We feel certain that, when fully mature, Elihu will learn to put this skill to the same use as have Eliphaz, Bildad, and Zophar: to distance himself emotionally from the sufferer through piety and self-righteousness.

Like the poem on wisdom, Elihu's speeches may be hard to justify within the dramatic structure of the book, and they may indeed have been added by a later editor. But however much Job may resemble a drama, that is not what it is; it is a collection of speeches in a narrative frame. Furthermore, we have already seen that the speeches in the dialogue, while not exactly thematically static, do not follow a strict dialectical pattern. The book works by concatenation. Within such a loose literary structure, the Elihu materials, whether original or not, do make sense as a complement to the chapters that are unquestionably part of the original book.

Elihu's fourth speech has a definite function in the unfolding of the poem's denouement, for when he has finished his lengthy description of the storm and the clearing that follows it, Yahweh Himself appears, the God traditionally associated with storms such as the one Elihu has just described. Job had insistently demanded that God appear to answer his complaints, had despaired of the confrontation, had fantasized about it, had feared it as he longed for it, but he had no power to compel it. But Elihu, the youthful, inexperienced, comical outsider, is able, through the sheer magic of his verse, to evoke Yahweh and compel His appearance. Those who demand drama may object to the presence of his speeches here; but by its placement, Elihu's speech is a convincing metaphor for the power of poetry, and thus partakes of the very essence of the book.

Thus evoked, Yahweh at last arrives with the book's denouement in the form of two speeches. He begins the first speech (chaps. 38–39) by addressing Job angrily without naming him, as if Job were beneath His notice, even though He is noticing him in such a dramatic fashion. Who was it, Yahweh asks, who conquered the ocean, fashioned the earth, determined its weather, and plumbed the sea? Does Job think he is capable of doing such things? Having begun His description of His own marvelous acts, Yahweh cannot stop. His view shifts from the great acts of cosmic control to the types of creatures He has created, and He goes on to describe a variety of animals. As He moves from creature to creature, His speech gradually loses its aggressive tone; God Himself seems to become more and more caught up in the contemplation of His own works, more and more engaged in His own poetic activity of describing them. By the time we reach the vulture, the last of the creatures described in God's first speech, we have quite forgotten what started it off, so pleased are we with the speech itself and the things it evokes.

Nowhere in the book is the poet's fascination with the fullness of life displayed more energetically than here, at the climax. His inclination to marvel at the world and at the life with which it teems, indulged until now in short, though numerous, bursts, is given full rein, so that it comes to overwhelm the book's problematics. Yahweh has no moral consolation to offer Job or mankind. Only He manages the universe; man cannot know how or by what rule He does so. All man has by way of consolation is whatever pleasure he can derive from life's sheer plenitude: wonder at God's creatures, amazement at His language, gratitude to be in a world so fascinating and abundant, no matter what suffering he has to endure in order to experience it. The intended effect of Yahweh's speech is to replace resentment with a sensation of the sublime. The point is made not by abstraction but by expression, because that is the only way it can be made. Poetry does not state the book's message, as it attempts to do in the Meditation on Wisdom; it *is* the book's message. Having heard Yahweh's poem, Job acknowledges his submission.

But Yahweh is not finished. His second speech (chaps. 40–41), after another angry preamble, takes up two last animals, mysterious beasts with mysterious names, often simply transliterated as Behemoth and Leviathan, but here translated as "the River Beast" and "the River Coiler." These creatures have the features of the hippopotamus and the crocodile, respectively, but unlike the animals in Yahweh's first speech, they are not portrayed naturalistically. The tone and character of the descriptions of them is almost mythic, as if the beasts were not actually a hippopotamus and a crocodile but monsters of the kind Yahweh had to contend with in order to create the world, in the manner of the ancient Near Eastern myths. They are liminal creatures, partaking of myth and reality, inhabiting both land and water. They are also of contrasting character, the River Beast being supremely placid and the River Coiler being supremely malevolent. As mysterious as the beasts is the language in which they are described; it is particularly opaque, especially when compared with the descriptions of the real animals in Yahweh's first speech, further evidence that the difficult language of the Book of Job is at least partly a deliberate expressive choice of the author's.

This second speech completes Yahweh's project of silencing Job, convincing him that the meaning and management of life are beyond his understanding. Yahweh's first speech was devoted to naturalistic descriptions of animals that Job might know from everyday life, of things he might delude himself into thinking he can understand but that God insists he cannot. God now confronts him with two creatures that are beyond all understanding, even beyond clear expression, two creatures both real and superreal that are not only beyond Job's control but beyond his ken. Job now sees that he and those he has lost and all mankind are really nothing at all compared with these beasts, let alone to Him who made them; his problems are nothing at all in the economy of the universe. Once again, the point is made not by reasoning, abstraction, or generalization, but by rhetoric and poetry. Job is now not merely silenced but overwhelmed. He recants his protests and at last accepts consolation for the dust and ashes he has lost, for the dust and ashes he is himself.

Such is the sequence of the argument of the Book of Job.

Approaching the book's structure historically, it seems clear that, like many books of the Bible, Job came into being in stages. Most scholars agree that the story of Job the Patient existed in some form prior to the present book, and that someone created the nucleus of the present Book of Job by adding the speeches of Job, his friends, and Yahweh. Either this author did not complete the third cycle of speeches or it was somehow corrupted in the course of transmission. To this basic Book of Job, many scholars maintain that later authors added the Meditation on Wisdom and the speeches of Elihu. Finally, some scholars maintain that the second speech of Yahweh is an afterthought by a later writer.

Even if the Book of Job as we have it is an accretion of parts modified and added over time, this need not preclude a reading that interprets the work as a coherent whole. The irregularities in the book's structure may be clues to the historical process by which it came into being, but they do not significantly undermine the book's literary coherence. There is no internal reason to assume that the three cycles of speeches were meant to be exactly symmetrical. Furthermore, other books of the Bible were composed by compiling earlier sources in ways that leave the seams showing, notably the Pentateuch and Jeremiah, yet these books have an evident plan that permits them to be read as coherent wholes.[12] In this introduction and in the notes to the translation, I make the strongest case I can for reading Job as a coherent work. The historical question of how it came to acquire its present form and which chapters or parts of chapters belong to the original book we can leave to source critics to debate.

Interpretation and Translation

Translators customarily preface their work with a statement of their approach to translation. But the translator of Job must first address the problem of interpretation, for before we can translate, it is necessary to decide what the text means, a particularly difficult task in the case of Job. We have seen that some of Job's obscurities may be part of the book's design. Sometimes a knotty passage will yield clues to the speaker's train of thought, but sometimes the difficulties do not yield to rereading alone.

To clarify these passages, we may look to the work of philologists who are specialists in the biblical text and in the cognate languages and literatures. Modern philological study has developed indispensable tools for the understanding of biblical Hebrew, and there is much that we understand about the text today that could not have been understood in earlier ages. But philological commentaries must be used with caution, for some apply their procedures in a mechanical way that is inappropriate to a poem, which calls for more latitude in interpretation than a legal text or a genealogical list.

When a philologist confronts a word that is not known from other Hebrew texts, or whose known meanings do not fit a particular passage, he finds meanings for its root or its cognates in other Semitic languages and plugs these into the questionable passage. This procedure often yields convincing results. If the problem does not yield to this type of solution, or if the text contains a grammatical or syntactic irregularity, the philologist tends to assume that the text has become corrupted over the centuries of transmission, and he attempts to "emend" it by reasoning what the author meant to say. This procedure, too, sometimes yields perfectly plausible results. The potential hazard of both methods is that, when used arbitrarily or in combination, the result can be a magic circle of improbability.

I have felt free to avail myself of emendations suggested by responsible modern commentators and even to propose one or two of my own, but only as a last resort, and only when the emendation is simple and plausible. I am more tolerant of emendations of vowels and word divisions than of consonantal emendations.[13] I call the reader's attention to emendations in the notes, but without going into detailed explanations that would necessitate a knowledge of Hebrew. I do not bother informing the reader of every case in which the translation takes a singular for a plural or a masculine for a feminine, because such irregularities can mostly be attributed to our imperfect understanding of the archaic syntax of the Book of Job and do not amount to emendations. I have tried to resist emendations that merely seem to improve an already intelligible text, even if the text is not completely smooth.[14] I have translated every word of the book, even those sometimes omitted as spurious or unintelligible; and I have rearranged verses as little as possible.[15]

The reason for my conservatism is a commitment to represent as accurately as possible both the literary culture within which the poet wrote and the poet's own literary imagination. Far removed from the Job-poet's world, we do not know his language as well as he did. Images and expressions that might seem to us bizarre, even impossible, might have struck his readers as perfectly intelligible. The discovery of Ugaritic and other ancient literatures of the Near East has clarified the meaning of many passages that earlier scholars wanted to emend or delete, giving hope that much else that remains obscure may eventually yield to future discoveries. More important, expressions that are apparently odd or unexpected may have been brilliant inventions of the author's that are hard for us to recognize or appreciate because of cultural differences or limitations of knowledge. The reason we read an ancient, exotic book is not to confirm our own literary habits and imaginations but to expand them. And the main reason we read a poem is not to gather information but to allow the poet's distinctive imagination to operate upon our own. Every time we propose to emend the text, we risk eliminating just what is distinctive about it.

My intention in making this translation of Job is to produce a poem in English that reflects the poetic values specific to biblical Hebrew and the original Book of Job. The author's imagery is inviolable, as that can always be reproduced in English, no matter how strange it may be. The balancing of clauses and the play of syntactic and semantic units of thought can also be approximately reproduced. The concision of biblical Hebrew cannot generally be reproduced in English, but the rhythmical relationships between clauses often can be; I have used a flexible accentual meter more as a help in indicating the rhythmical balance of the original than as a bow to the conventions of English verse. I have used indentation to suggest the relationships between parallel clauses. I have tried to indicate the rhetorical texture of the original, even at the risk of occasionally using language that sounds odd in English, when I thought the author went out of his way for a particular effect. As for the more subjective matter of tone, I have at least been conscious of it and can only hope that some of it comes through.

I have tried to identify in each line just what it is that the original poet thought made his work a poem, and, whatever else had to be altered, to convey that essential thing (or, in the hard cases, those essential things) in English. I have tried to let the text suggest its own translation and to interfere as little as possible. I have avoided imposing arbitrary flights of imagination on the Book of Job's text, for I have a horror of the free-and-easy approach to translation. Often I have used the philologists as my disciplinarians, letting them tell me what was a reasonable interpretation and what was too far a stretch.

The result does not have to sound exactly like English. Part of the pleasure of reading an ancient text lies in its exoticism. I have not gone out of my way to stress the book's foreignness, but neither have I tried to disguise it. I have adopted a register of English somewhat higher than that of ordinary prose, since the Hebrew is decidedly not colloquial, even for biblical times.

The translation is followed by notes. Their main purpose is to clarify the argument of the book and to make explicit the train of thought within the chapters. The notes also explain some of the Book of Job's allusions to ancient Near Eastern lore, to artifacts of ancient life, and to matters of fact that the ancient book's author could count on his audience to know. Sometimes they simply point out some feature of the text that I think the reader might like having called to his attention. The notes register emendations and occasionally explain briefly the reasoning that led me to a nonstandard interpretation of a difficult passage. They do not go into philological detail; Hebraists will be able to reconstruct my reasoning on their own or by checking the commentaries I consulted. I do not ordinarily provide alternative interpretations in the notes, but I have done so in a few cases, such as those described earlier in this introduction, where the structure of the book is at issue. In such cases, I generally adopt a harmonizing approach. I also provide an alternative explanation for the reader who finds my reasoning forced.

I often felt, as I worked, like a religious scribe writing a Torah scroll for use in the synagogue. Such a scribe is required to read each word aloud from the printed page before writing it down with his quill or reed pen, and if he is not certain that a letter he has written is perfectly clear, he has to test it by showing it to an average schoolchild. (The idea is that the average schoolchild will read exactly what the scribe has written, for better or worse, and will not be inclined merely to recite the word correctly from memory, as someone more learned might do.) I have tried to be that conscientious in carrying out my responsibility as a mediator of a canonical text of Western literature and religion. I have aimed for a disciplined translation that follows as closely as possible the standard Hebrew text of Job and adheres as closely as possible to meanings that can reasonably be attributed to Hebrew words and, above all, to the poetic values that I thought were important to the author. I imagined him reading over my shoulder as I wrote and shaking his head with annoyance when I was about to take too great a liberty.

Notes to the Introduction

1. That the story of Job existed before the present Book of Job is a topic of debate among scholars, as is every aspect of the history and interpretation of Job. In this introduction, I simply present the opinions that seem most likely to me; the reader who wishes to become better informed about the range of scholarly opinion and the reasons for the various positions can consult the books and commentaries cited in the bibliography. But I strongly recommend that before doing so, he familiarize himself thoroughly with the actual text of the book.

2. Ezek. 14:14, 20. Danel (spelled without an "i") in these verses is not the biblical character Daniel but a legendary hero like the Danel of the Ugaritic epic of Aqhat.

3. James 5:11.

4. Sura 21:83–84 and 38:40/41–44.

5. Joshua: "After the death of Moses"; Judges: "After the death of Joshua"; Isaiah: "The vision of Isaiah . . . which he saw in the days of Uzziah"; Ruth: "In the days when the Judges ruled," etc.

6. There is, however, one passage in the book (31:26–28) that reflects a distinctly monotheistic background. This inconsistency may be a slip on the author's part, perhaps because the part of the speech in which it occurs was adapted from a preexisting work or literary tradition.

7. The Sumerian story in Samuel Noah Kramer, *History Begins at Sumer* (Garden City, N.Y.: Doubleday, 1959), pp. 114–18; "Egyptian Dispute on Suicide," in James Bennett Pritchard, ed., *Ancient Near Eastern Texts Relating to the Old Testament*, 2d ed. (Princeton: Princeton University Press, 1955), pp. 405–7 (customarily referred to as ANET); "Tale of the Eloquent Peasant," in ANET, pp. 407–10; "I Will Praise the Lord of Wisdom," in ANET, pp. 434–37; "Babylonian Theodicy," in ANET, pp. 438–40.

8. The Wisdom of Ben Sira (also known as Ecclesiasticus) is a Hebrew book containing poetic maxims, didactic poems, and

psalms, written in Palestine about 170 B.C. The Wisdom of Solomon is an exposition of the Jewish religion in terms of Hellenistic philosophy, written in Greek in the first century B.C., probably in Alexandria. Both Ben Sira and the Wisdom of Solomon are considered canonical by Roman Catholics, apocryphal by Jews and Protestants.

9. Strictly speaking, only a bit over half the book is part of the dialogue: chapters 4–27. The other poems are individual statements by Job, the author, Elihu, and God, to which there is no reply.

10. Such poetic excurses are generally set off typographically in the translation. Discrepancies between these set pieces and other parts of the book are indications that the former may derive from earlier works; alternatively, they may employ a stylized manner of expression without taking the exact circumstances into consideration. For an example, see the note to 19:17.

11. I owe this observation to my friend and colleague Professor S. A. Geller.

12. The order of incoherence is completely different in the present Isaiah, a biblical book that does not permit such a unifying reading. Each of its two parts is composed of separate historical layers, but the two parts themselves cannot be harmonized by any literary approach.

13. The reason for conceding less authority to the vowels than to the consonants is that the system of writing employed by the original author of Job indicated only the consonants. The vowels were added, in the form of little dots and dashes over, under, and inside the consonants, more than a thousand years later, and therefore may be assumed not to be an authoritative representation of the author's intention.

14. As in 3:22, where the Hebrew word *gil* (joy) is commonly emended to *gal* (mound), yielding the translation "who rejoice about the burial mound." This emendation does create parallelism between the first half of the line and the second half, which reads "thrill to find the grave." But not every verse of biblical Hebrew verse contains two parallel clauses, and the text as it stands makes good sense; literally, it means "who rejoice alongside happiness," here translated as "whose joy exceeds mere happiness." Such a use of the preposition *el* is not standard, but it is documented elsewhere, and odd usages of common words are quite usual in Job.

15. Chapter numbers and every fifth verse number are indicated in the margin. In the few places where verses have been rearranged, additional chapter and verse numbers appear for the reader's orientation.

THE
BOOK
OF
JOB

The Story of Job

A man once lived in the land of Utz. His name was Job. This 1:1
man was <u>innocent</u>, <u>upright</u>, and <u>God-fearing</u>, and <u>kept</u>
<u>himself apart from</u> evil. Seven sons and three daughters were
born to him. His flock consisted of seven thousand sheep,
three thousand camels, five hundred yoke of oxen, five hundred female donkeys, and a large staff of servants. He was the
greatest of the men of the East.

His sons would make a feast each year, each one in his own
house by turns, and they would invite their three sisters to
eat and drink with them. When the days of the feast would 1:5
come round, Job would send to purify them, rising early in
the morning to offer wholeburnt offerings, one for each.
For Job thought, "Perhaps my sons have sinned by cursing
God in their hearts." Job did this every year.

One day, the lesser gods came to attend upon Yahweh,
and the Accuser came among them. Yahweh said to the
Accuser, "Where are you coming from?" and the Accuser
answered Yahweh, "From roving and roaming about the
world." Yahweh said to the Accuser, "Have you taken note
of my servant Job, for there is no one like him on earth:
innocent, upright, and God-fearing, and keeping himself
apart from evil." The Accuser answered Yahweh, "Is Job
God-fearing for nothing? Look how You have sheltered 1:10
him on all sides, him and his household and everything he
has, and have blessed everything he does, so that his cattle
have spread out all over the land. But reach out with Your

hand and strike his property, and watch him curse You to Your face!"

Yahweh said to the Accuser, "Everything he has is in your power, but do not harm his person."

The Accuser took his leave of Yahweh.

One day, when his sons and daughters were feasting and drinking wine in the house of the eldest brother, a messenger came to Job and said, "The cattle were plowing and the donkeys were grazing by their side and Sabeans fell on them and seized them and killed the servants with their swords, and only I got away to tell you!"

1:15

While he was speaking, another came and said, "A fearful fire fell from heaven and burned up the sheep and the servants and consumed them, and only I got away to tell you!"

While he was speaking, another came and said, "The Chaldeans formed into three companies and came at the camels from all directions and took them and killed the servants with their swords, and only I got away to tell you!"

While he was speaking, another came and said, "Your sons and daughters were eating and drinking wine in the house of the eldest brother and a great wind came from across the desert and struck the four corners of the house and it fell on the young people and they died, and only I got away to tell you!"

1:20

Job got up and tore his robe and shaved his head and flung himself to the ground and lay there prostrate and said,

"Naked I came from my mother's womb
and naked I return there.
Yahweh has given and Yahweh has taken.
Blessed be the name of Yahweh."

In spite of everything, Job did not sin and did not attach blame to God.

One day, the lesser gods came to attend upon Yahweh, *2:1* and among them came the Accuser to attend upon Yahweh. Yahweh said to the Accuser, "Where are you coming from?" and the Accuser answered Yahweh, "From roving and roaming about the world." Yahweh said to the Accuser, "Have you taken note of my servant Job, for there is no one like him on earth: innocent, upright, and God-fearing, and keeping himself apart from evil; he even persists in his innocence, though you prevailed upon me to ruin him for no reason!" The Accuser answered Yahweh,

"Skin protecting skin! A man will give whatever he has for the sake of his own life. But reach out with Your hand and *2:5* strike his person, his flesh, and watch him curse You to Your face!"

Yahweh said to the Accuser, "He is in your power, but see that you preserve his life."

The Accuser took his leave of Yahweh and smote Job with sickening eruptions from the soles of his feet to the crown of his head. Job took a shard to scrape himself with and sat down in ashes. His wife said to him, "Are you still persisting in your innocence? Curse God and die!"

He said to her, "You are speaking like a disgraceful *2:10* woman! Should we accept the good from God and not accept the bad?" In spite of everything, Job did not sin with his lips.

Job's three friends heard about all the trouble that had come upon him, and each one came from his own place: Eliphaz the Temanite, Bildad the Shuhite, and Zophar the

Naamatite. They agreed to meet to go and to mourn with him and comfort him. Peering from the distance, they could not recognize him. They raised their voices and wept, and each tore his robe, and all put dirt on their heads, throwing it heavenward. Seven days and seven nights they sat with him on the ground, none saying a word to him, for they saw that his pain was very great.

Job's Curse

Then Job spoke and cursed his day and raised his voice and 3:1
said:

Blot out the day when I was born
    and the night that said, "A male has been conceived!"
Make that day dark!
    No god look after it from above,
    no light flood it.
Foul it, darkness, deathgloom; 3:5
    rain-clouds settle on it;
    heat-winds turn it to horror.
Black take that night!
    May it not count in the days of the year,
    may it not come in the round of the months.
That night be barren! That night!
    No joy ever come in it!
Curse it, men who spell the day,
    men skilled to stir Leviathan.
May its morning stars stay dark,
    may it wait for light in vain,
    never look on the eyelids of dawn—
because it did not lock the belly's gates 3:10
    and curtain off my eyes from suffering.

Why did I not die inside the womb,
    or, having left it, give up breath at once?

Why did knees advance to greet me,
    or breasts, for me to suck?
Now I would be lying quietly;
    I would be sleeping then, at rest,
with kings and counselors of the earth,
    men who build rubble heaps for themselves,
3:15 or with princes, men with gold,
    men who fill their tombs with silver.
Why was I not like a stillbirth, hidden,
    like infants who never saw the light?
There the wicked cease their troubling,
    there the weary are at rest,
where the captives have repose,
    and need not heed the foreman's voice;
where the humble and the great are,
    the slave, now free, beside his lord.

3:20 Why is the sufferer given light?
    Why life, to men who gag on bile,
who wait for a death that never comes,
    though they would rather dig for it than gold;
whose joy exceeds mere happiness,
    thrill to find the grave?
Why, to a man whose way is hidden,
    because a god has blocked his path?
For my sighs are brought to me for bread,
    and my cries poured out for water.
3:25 One thing I feared, and it befell,
    and what I dreaded came to me.
No peace had I, nor calm, nor rest;
    but torment came.

Eliphaz's First Speech

4:1
Eliphaz the Temanite then took up the argument and said:

Might one try a word with you, or would you tire?—
    But who could hold back words now?
You were always the one to instruct the many,
    to strengthen failing hands;
your words would pick up men who had fallen
    and firm up buckling knees;
yet now it is your turn, and you go faint; 4:5
    it has reached you, and you are undone.

Isn't your innocence some reassurance?
    Doesn't your righteousness offer you hope?
Think: What really guiltless man has gone under?
    Where have the upright perished?
I see men plowing wickedness,
    seeding, harvesting trouble—
one breath from God and they perish;
    one snort from Him and they're gone.
The lion roars! Listen! The lion!— 4:10
    The lion's teeth are cracked.
    The lion wanders, finds no prey.
    Young lions scatter.

Now, word has reached me in stealth—
    my ear caught only a snatch of it—
in wisps of thought, night visions,

when slumber drifts down upon men.
Fear came over me, fear and a shudder,
　　every bone in me shook.
4:15　Then—a gust crossing my face,
bristling the hairs on my skin,
and there he was standing—I could not make him out—
a shape before my eyes—
Hush! I hear his voice:
　　"Can man be more righteous than God,
　　　　or purer than He who made him?
　　God does not trust His own courtiers,
　　　　sees folly in His own angels;
　　what then of dwellers in houses of clay,
　　　　their foundations sunk in the dirt,
　　that crumble before the moth,
4:20　　　　crack into shards between morning and evening,
　　　　　　perish forever, not even aware of their fate?
　　See how their wealth wanders away with them,
　　　　how they die without wisdom.
5:1　Go, cry out your rage—but who will answer?
　　　　Which of the angels would you implore?
Remember: Only fools are killed by anger,
　　only simpletons by jealous fury.

I have seen a fool strike roots;
snap! I cursed his house:
Now his sons are far from help,
　　crushed in the public square;
　　no one came to their rescue.
5:5　Now the hungry dine on his harvest,

Eliphaz / words of wisdom

Keeping Job from temptation

while he has to scrabble for it among thorns,
and thirsty men gulp his wealth.
Remember: Evil does not emerge from the soil,
   or trouble sprout from the ground.
Man was born to trouble
as sparks dart to the sky."

Original Sin

No, I look to El,
   entrust my affairs to the care of a god
who makes things great beyond man's grasp,
   and wonders beyond any numbering;
who puts the rain on the face of the earth,
   sends water to the countryside;
raises the humble to the heights,
   lifts gloomy men to rescue;
spoils the plans of cunning men,
   so their hands can do nothing clever;
traps the shrewd in their own cunning,
   makes the schemer's plotting seem like rashness
(by day they stumble against the darkness,
   grope in midday as if it were night);
who saves the poor from the knife,
   from the maw, from the mighty,
so that the humble have hope,
   and evil has to shut its mouth.

+ Positive +

5:10

5:15

Yes, happy the man whom God reproves!
Do not reject Shaddai's correction.
   He may give pain, but He binds the wound;
   He strikes, but His hands bring healing.

In six-times-trouble He will save you;
in seven, no harm will touch you.

5:20   He will rescue you from death in dearth,
            from sword in war.
        When the tongue's lash snaps, you will be well hidden,
        have nothing to fear when raiders arrive.
            Raiders and famine will make you smile,
            wild beasts give you nothing to fear.
        The stones in the field will be your allies;
        predators will yield to you.
            You will be sure of peace in your household;
            visit it when you like—you will not fail!
5:25   Then, be assured of plentiful seed,
        of offspring like the earth's green shoots.
            Still robust you will reach the grave,
            like sheaves heaped high in their season.
        All this we have studied and know it is so.
        Think it over; take it to heart!

Job's Reply to Eliphaz's First Speech

Job answered:

6:1

If there were some way to weigh my rage,
  if my disaster would fit in a balance,
they would drag down the ocean's sands;
that is why my speech is clumsy.
For Shaddai's arrows are all around me—
  my breath absorbs their venom—
    terror of the god invests me.

  Is that a wild ass braying over his grass?—
  an ox bellowing over his feed?
  Who can eat unsalted food?
  What flavor is there in the drool of mallows?
  I have no appetite to touch them;
  they are as nauseous as my flesh!

6:5

If only what I ask would happen—
if some god would grant my hope—
if that god would consent to crush me,
loose his hand and crack me open—
even that would comfort me
(though I writhed in pain unsparing),
for never have I suppressed the Holy One's commands.

6:10

  What strength have I to go on hoping?
  How far off is my end,

even if I live long?
Have I the bearing-strength of rock? Is my flesh bronze?
Is there no help within myself?
Has common sense been driven from me
to one who holds back kindnesses from friends,
to one who has lost the fear of Shaddai?

6:15   As for my friends—
they failed me like a riverbed,
wandered off, like water in a wadi.
    Gloomy on an icy day,
    covered up with snow;
    they flow one moment, then are gone;
    when it is hot, they flicker away.
    Their dry courses twist,
    wander into wasteland, vanish.
      Caravans from Tema peer;
        Sabean trains move toward them, hoping:
6:20   Disappointment for their trust—
        they reach them, find frustration.
    That is how you are to me:
    You see terror, take fright yourselves.

When have I said to you, "Give me, give"?
"Bribe someone for me with your wealth"?
"Save me from my enemy"?
"Pay my ransom to some tyrant"?
All I ask is that you teach me—
I will listen quietly:
Tell me what I have done wrong!

[handwritten marginal note: Job has been left alone, abandoned by friends]

How eloquent are honest words—   6:25
How then can you teach effectively?
Do you think you can teach me with words?
Is a speech of despair just wind?
Would you also divide an orphan's goods by lot
and haggle over your neighbor's property?

And now, be good enough to turn toward me—
  See if I lie to your faces.
Come back! You'll find no evil here—
  Come back!—only my vindication.
Is there error on my tongue?
  What am I speaking of except disaster?   6:30

Man's life on earth is a term of indenture;   7:1
  his days are like a laborer's,
a slave, who pants for a little shade,
  a day laborer, who only wants his wages.
I too am granted blank moons;
  troubled nights have been my lot.
When I lie down, I say,
  "How soon can I get up?"
    The night time stretches,
and I have tossing and turning enough to last till dawn.
My flesh is covered with worms and dirty scabs;   7:5
  my skin is cracked and oozing.
My days are swifter than a weaver's shuttle;
  they end when the thread of hope gives out.
Remember: My life is just a breath;
my eye will never again see pleasure.

return to hear my pleas.

lack of God's presence

The questing eye will not detect me;
Your eye will catch me—just!—
   and I'll be gone.

A cloud dissipates, vanishes,
and once below the ground
no man comes up again;
7:10 he never goes back to his home;
   his place no longer knows him.

Job has been diminished to nonexistence — rejected by life

Why should I restrain my mouth?—
   I speak from a dejected spirit,
     complain out of sheer bitterness:
Am I Yamm-ocean or the Serpent,
that You post a guard over me?
I tell myself, "My couch will comfort me,
   my bed will bear a part of my complaint,"
only to have You frighten me with nightmares,
   panic me with visions of the night;
7:15   I'd rather choke—
  death is better than this misery.

Why should I stay loyal

I've had enough! I will not live forever!
Let me alone; my life is just a breath.
What is man that You make so much of him,
   and think about him so,
examine him each morning,
   appraise him every moment?
How long till You turn away from me
long enough for me to swallow my own spit?
7:20 I have sinned: But what have I done to You,

keeper, jailer of men?
Why should You make me Your target,
    a burden to myself?
Why not forgive my crimes,
    and pardon me my sin?
In no time, I'll be lying in the earth;
    when You come looking for me, I'll be gone.

at this rate I'll be gone by the time my God returns to me

Bildad's First Speech

8:1 Bildad the Shuhite then took up the argument and said:

How long will you go on like this?
　What a great wind are the words from your mouth!
Would El pervert judgment?
　Would Shaddai pervert what is right?
Your sons have sinned against Him, that is all,
　　and He got rid of them
　　on account of their own crimes.
8:5 If you would now seek out the god,
　　beseech Shaddai,
　　　be pure and true—
　　He would rouse Himself for you,
　　restore your righteous home.
Your former life will seem a paltry thing,
　so greatly will you prosper in the end.

Just ask the older generation,
　and set your mind to questioning *their* fathers
(for we are no older than yesterday
　and do not really know;
　our days on earth are only shadows):
8:10 They will teach you,
　　they will tell you,
　　　they will bring words up from memory.
Can papyrus grow tall without a marsh

or reeds flourish without water?
Still in flower,

not yet cut,

even before the grass,

it withers.

Such is the fate of all who put God out of mind;

thus the hope of the wicked man fades,

whatever he trusts in fails.

He puts his trust in a spider's web,

leans on his house, but it does not stand;   8:15

grasps at it, but it does not hold.

Juicy green before the sun,

his suckers creep over his planting bed,

his roots tangle-twist a rock heap,

he clutches a house of stones.

But let him be snatched from his place,

and his place denies him: "I know you not!"

Such is his happy lot—

others sprout from that dirt. . . .

cannot even finish the sentence

No, God would not reject the innocent,   8:20

would not take hold of a bad man's hand.

He will yet fill your mouth with laughter,

fill your lips with cries of joy.

Your foe will yet be clothed in shame,

the wicked untented.

Job's Reply to Bildad's First Speech

9:1 Job answered:

True, I know that this is so;
but can a mortal beat a god at law?
If someone chose to challenge Him,
He would not answer even the thousandth part!
Shrewd or powerful one may be,
but who has faced Him hard and come out whole?

9:5 He moves the mountains and they are unaware,
    overturns them in His rage.
He shakes the earth from its place;
    its pillars totter.
He orders the sun not to rise,
    seals up the stars.
He stretches out the heavens all alone,
    and treads Yamm's back.
He makes the Pleiades, Orion, and the Bear,
    the South Wind's chambers.

9:10 He makes things great beyond man's grasp,
    and wonders beyond any numbering.
Yet when He comes my way, I do not notice;
    He passes on, and I am unaware.

If He should seize a thing, who could restore it?
    Who could say to Him, "What are You doing?"

A god could not avert His anger—
    Rahab's cohorts bent beneath Him—
how then could I raise my voice at Him,
    or choose to match my words with His?
Even if I were right, I could not answer,
    could only plead with my opponent;
and if I summoned Him, and if He answered me,
    I doubt that He would listen to my voice,
since He crushes me for just a hair,
    and bruises me for nothing,
will not let me catch my breath,
    feeds me full of poison.
Is it power? He is mighty!
Is it judgment? Who can summon Him?
I may be righteous, but my mouth convicts me;
    innocent, yet it makes me seem corrupt.
I *am* good.
I do not know myself.
I hate my life.
It is all one; and so I say,
"The good and the guilty He destroys alike."
If some scourge brings sudden death,
    He mocks the guiltless for their melting hearts;
some land falls under a tyrant's sway—
    He veils its judges' faces;
if not He, then who?

But I—
my days are lighter than a courier's feet;

9:15

9:20

9:25

His anger transforms into

they flee and never see a moment's joy;
they dart away as if on skiffs of reed,
swift as a vulture swooping to his food.

I tell myself to give up my complaining,
    put aside my sullenness and breathe a while;
but still I fear my suffering,
knowing You will never count me innocent.
I am always the one in the wrong—
why should I struggle in vain?

9:30   Even if I bathed in liquid snow
    and purified my palms with lye,
You would just dip me in a ditch—
    my very clothes would find me sickening.

Scholar. opinion betrayal.

For a man like me cannot just challenge Him,
"Let's go to court together!"
Now if there were an arbiter between us
to lay his hand on both of us,
    to make Him take His rod away,
    so that His terror would not cow me,
9:35   then I could speak without this fear of Him;
    for now I am not steady in His presence.

10:1   I am fed up with my life;
    I might as well complain with all abandon,
    and put my bitter spirit into words.
So to the god I say, "Do not condemn me!
Just tell me what the accusation is!
Do You get pleasure from harassing,

hopelessfaith

    spurning what You wore Yourself out making,
    shining on the councils of the wicked?
Do You have eyes of flesh?
    Do You see as mortals do?
Is Your life span the same as any human's,   10:5
    Your years like those of ordinary men,
that You come seeking out my every sin
    and leave no fault of mine unpunished—
knowing I've done nothing truly wicked,
    that nothing can be rescued from Your hands?

Your hands shaped me, kneaded me
together, round about—
    and now would You devour me?
Remember, You kneaded me like clay;
    will You turn me back to dirt?
Just look: 10:10
You poured me out like milk,
    You curdled me like cheese;
You covered me with flesh and skin,
    wove me a tangle of sinews and bones,
gave me life, a gift,
    sustained my breath with Your command.
Yet all these things You stored up in Your heart—
I know how Your mind works!
When I do sin, You keep Your eye on me,
and You would never clear me of my guilt.
If I do wrong, too bad for me!   10:15
But even when I'm good I cannot raise my head,
so filled with shame,

Connection to the build of humans

so drenched with my own misery.
Proud as a lion You stalk me
and then withdraw,
pleased with Yourself for what You've done to me.
You keep Your enmity toward me fresh,
    work up Your anger at me;
so my travail is constantly renewed.

Why did You ever take me from the womb?
I could have died, and no eye had to see.
I could have been as if I never were,
hauled from belly to grave.

10:20   But as it is, my days are few, so stop!
Let me alone so I can catch my breath
before I go my way, not to return,
into a land of dark and deathgloom,
land obscure as any darkness,
land of deathgloom, land of chaos,
where You blaze forth in rays of black!"

Zophar's First Speech

Zophar the Naamatite then took up the argument and said: 11:1

Should a speech go unanswered just because it is long?
    Is someone with ready lips always right?
You want to silence people with your bluster,
    cow them with sarcasm, no one restrains you.
You say, "My teaching's perfect," "I was pious"—
Yes, in *your* eyes.

But how I wish the god would speak,   11:5
    open His lips when you are present,
    tell you some of wisdom's mysteries
(for wisdom comes wrapped up in double folds)—
then you would realize:
The god is punishing you less than you deserve.

Can you find out God's depths,
    or find the outer limits of Shaddai?
What can you do at the heavens' height?
    What can you know that is deeper than Sheol,
    greater than the earth's extension, wider than the sea?
Should He pass by, confine, or confiscate,   11:10
who could restore?
He knows which men are false;
    could He see wrong and look the other way?
Yet hollow-core man thinks he has some wisdom—
man, born no better than a saddle-ass or onager.

doesn't repeat anything.

If you would only set your mind,
  stretch out your hands to Him,
get rid of anything you own through crime,
  and harbor nothing wrongly gotten in your home—

11:15 then you could hold your head up, blameless,
  be rock-solid, fearing nothing.
Then you would put your troubles out of mind,
  remember them no more than water
  vanished from a wadi.
Your earthbound days would rise as high as noon,
  and darkness turn to morning.
You'd live in confidence, with hope,
  dig your burrow, lie secure,
  crouch there, fearing no one.
Multitudes would seek your favor,

11:20 while the wicked gaze with longing eyes,
  all refuge lost to them,
  their hopes all spent in sighs.

Job's Reply to Zophar's First Speech

Job answered: 12:1

What a distinguished tribe you are!
    All wisdom dies with you!
But I too have a mind.
I am no less a man than you;
    and who does *not* have such ideas as these?
I am one who gives his neighbors cause to smile:
    "He calls to God and He answers him!"—
    a laughingstock—righteous, innocent.
Smug men's minds hold scorn for disaster,   12:5
    ready for anyone who stumbles.
Highway robbers' families lie tranquil;
    men who anger El are confident
    of what the god has brought into their hands.

But just ask the animals—they will instruct you;
    the birds of heaven—they will tell.
Or speak to the earth and it will instruct you,
    the fish of the ocean will tell you the tale:
Who of all these is not aware
that Yahweh's hand has done all this,
the hand that controls every living soul,   12:10
    the breath of every man made of flesh?

"The ear," they say, "is the best judge of speech,
    the palate knows what food is tasty."
    "Wisdom," they say, "belongs to elders;
    length of years makes a man perspicacious."
He has wisdom and power;
    He has counsel and insight.
If He tears down, there is no rebuilding;
    if He confines, there is no release.

12:15 If He blocks the water, the water dries up;
    but if He lets it loose,
    it overturns the earth.
Both skill and might are with Him;
    He owns both those who do wrong
    and those who lead others astray.
He makes counselors go mad and judges rave,
    unties the bonds of kings,
    (though He Himself had bound the sash about their waists).
He makes the priests go mad,
    and gives eternal truths the lie.

12:20 He strips the ready counselors of speech,
    makes off with the elders' reason,
heaps scorn on nobles,
    weakens the pride of the mighty.
He discloses deep things out of darkness,
    brings deathdark to the light.
He elevates some nations, then destroys them,
    spreads traps for other nations,
    but guides them safely through.
He strips the peoples' leaders of their judgment,

sends them off-course in a trackless wasteland,
   groping in the darkness, lightless,   12:25
   wandering crazily like drunken men.

Look, there is nothing my eye hasn't seen,   13:1
   nothing my ear hasn't heard and taken in,
   nothing that you know that I do not.
      I am no less a man than you.
But I would speak to Shaddai,
   I want to dispute with El,
while you are merely smearers, liars,
   mountebanks, every one of you.
If only you would just be quiet!—   13:5
   In you, that would be wisdom!

Listen to my accusation,
   pay heed to my lips' complaint.
Will you speak falsehood for the sake of El,
   and speak deceit on His account?
Will you show partiality to Him,
   argue on El's behalf?
How would it be if He questioned you?
   Could you play Him for a fool, as you do with people?
He is sure to reprimand you,   13:10
   if you behave with secret partiality.
Think how you would panic if He were to loom,
   and all His fearsomeness came down on you:
   Your memory would turn to ashes,
      your bodies, into lumps of clay.

[Handwritten annotations: "Don't try to think you are better." "Ok. That's sinning" "His friends are accusing him and he rebukes that they are lying on behalf of God."]

He is reaching a breaking point

Be silent in my presence! I will speak,
  and let whatever happens to me happen.
Why am I carrying my body in my teeth,
  my life-breath in my hands?

13:15 Let Him kill me!—I will never flinch,
  but will protest His conduct to His face,
and He Himself will be my vindication,
  for flatterers can never come before Him.

You've done something much worse

Listen, all who hear me, to my speech,
  my declaration in your ears:
I am laying out my case,
knowing I am in the right.
Who would contend with me?—
I will shut my mouth at once and die.

13:20 Only two things do not do to me,
and then I will not hide from You:
Take Your palm away from me,
  and do not cow me with the fear of You.
Then You can call, and I will answer,
or I will speak and You can answer me.
How many are my sins and my offenses?
  Advise me of my crimes and sins.
Why do You hide Your face,
  regard me as Your enemy?

13:25 Would You tyrannize a driven leaf
  or hound a shriveled straw,
that You record my every bitter deed,

charge me with my boyhood sins?
Is that why You put my feet in stocks,
    watch my every step,
    mark the roots of my feet?

Man born of woman: *14:1*
His days are few, his belly full of rage.
He blooms and withers like a blossom,
    flees, unlingering, like a shadow,
    wears out like a rotten thing,   *13:28*
    a cloth moth-eaten.
Do You really keep a watch on such a thing?
    Do You call a man like me
    to judgment against You?

Who can purify a thing impure?
No one!
If his years are predetermined,   *14:5*
    and You control the number of his months,
    and You have set him bounds he cannot cross—
just turn away from him and let him be!
Let him work off his contract,
day laborer that he is.

Even a tree has hope:
If you cut it, it sprouts again.
Its suckers never fail.
Its roots may grow old in the earth,
    its stump may die in the ground,

but just the smell of water makes it bud
and put out branches like a sapling.

14:10   But man, when he wearies and dies,
      when a human gives out—where is he then?
Water vanishes from a lake,
      rivers dry up parched,
and man lies down and does not rise;
they will not wake till the skies disappear;
      they will not rise from their sleep.

If You would only hide me in Sheol,
      conceal me till Your anger passes,
      set me a term and then remember me
      (but if a person dies, how can he live?),
I could endure my term in hope,
until my time came round to sprout again.

14:15   Then You would call, and I would answer,
      when You longed to see Your handiwork.
But as it is, You count my every step,
      see nothing but my sins.
My sin is sealed up in a bundle,
      and You attached the seal.

Yes, the mountain collapses and wears away;
      the cliff is dislodged from its place;
stones are scoured by water into dust,
      torrents wash away earth's soil—
         and You destroy man's hopes.

14:20   You assault him and he vanishes forever;
      You turn his face dark and send him away.

His sons become great and he never knows,
    or else they fail, and he never finds out.
All he knows is his own body's ache;
he mourns himself alone.

Eliphaz's Second Speech

15:1   Eliphaz the Temanite then took up the argument and said:

What a wise man, uttering windy wisdom
   out of a bellyful of hot air from the East,
instructing with useless speeches
   and words that have no value!
That's you: subverting piety,
   laying unworthy complaints before the god.

15:5   Guilt is what has schooled your mouth,
   and so you choose devious language.
Your own mouth proclaims your guilt, not I;
   your own lips speak out against you.
Were you born first of all mankind?
   Were you brought forth before the hills?
Did you overhear the gods in council,
   snatch away some wisdom for yourself?
What do you know that we do not?
   What do you grasp that we have missed?

15:10   There are gray-haired, aged men among us,
   men years older than your father!
Are pious consolations and a softly spoken word
   so trivial in your opinion?
How could you let your heart sweep you away
   and let your eyes beguile you
to render such a windy speech to El,
   and let your mouth emit such words?

How can mortal man be guiltless?

How can woman's brood be innocent?

He does not trust His own angels, 15:15

does not find even the heavens guiltless!—

What must He think of foul and disgusting

man, who guzzles sin like water? *Damn. Hypocrisy*

Let me tell you—pay attention!—

let me speak of things revealed to me,

things that wise men used to tell, did not withhold,

that they had gotten from their fathers

(men who were granted the land for themselves,

men among whom no stranger wandered):

All the days of the wicked man, 15:20

however many years are in store for the tyrant,

he writhes, tormented.

The sound of fear is in his ears;

plunderers overtake him in peacetime;

not sure how to get home for the darkness,

certain the sword is upon him;

he wanders wondering where bread is,

certain the dark day is at hand,

in terror that straits and hardship will rush him,

braced, like a king for an army's assault.

All this for lifting his hand against El, 15:25

for trying his might against Shaddai;

for charging against Him, neck taut

behind his thick-bossed shields;

If the gods so wish, you will be worse off

for burying his face in his own fat,
   and putting thickness on his loins.
He dwells in ruined cities,
   uninhabitable houses
      already half turned to rubble.
He will not have wealth,
   nor will his fortune endure;
      his fullness will never weigh him to the ground.
15:30 Never will he escape the darkness.
Flame dries up his shoots;
   his own breath blows them away.
(Let no one trust deceiving falsehood,
   for falsehood is its own return.)
He withers before his day is over,
   his boughs not lush;
he drops his still-unripe fruit, like a vine,
   casts his blossoms like an olive tree.
Barren indeed is the throng of the godless;
   the bribe-takers' homes are wasted by fire—
15:35 men conceiving trouble, bearing sin
   out of bellies that breed deceit.

Job's Reply to Eliphaz's Second Speech

Job answered:

I have heard plenty of this kind before.
Clumsy comforters you are, all three!
Are windy words ever exhausted?
What is tormenting you,
that you feel you have to speak?
I can speak as well as you.
If you were in my place,
I would compose a speech about you,
    shake my head in sorrow for you,
    use my mouth to wish you strength,
    spare my lips no mumbling motion.
Now, if I speak, my pain does not let up,
    and if I stop, it does not leave me.
        Now it has worn me out.

16:5

You have wiped out all my company,
crumpled me; my witness is
my own emaciation, rising in witness against me.

He rends me in his rage, reviles me,
    grinds his teeth at me; my foe
        sharpens his eyes' blade at me.

[handwritten annotation:] Nah. He was accused of the same

[handwritten annotation:] Job is starting to get self-conscious

16:10   They open their maws at me,
            slap my cheeks to shame me,
                crowd around me, menacing.

        El hands me over to evil men,
            tosses me into the wicked man's clutches.
        I was at peace when He shard-shattered me,
            grabbed me by the neck, crack-crumbled me,
                set me up as a target for shooting.
        His arrow-men surrounded me,
            split my gut without a qualm,
                spilled my life-juices on the ground.
        He breaks through me, breach on breach;
            rushes at me like a champion.
16:15   I have sewn a hemp shirt to my skin,
            dug my horns into the dirt.
        My face is flushed with weeping;
            on my fluttering eyelids, deathdark—
        but not because I hold goods gained through violence,
            and though my prayer is pure.
        O Earth! Do not conceal my blood!
            And may my cry not find a place to rest!
        Even now, my witness is in heaven,
            my corroboration is on high.

16:20   Such advocates! Such friends!
        My eye drips godward.
        A man might as well dispute with a god
        as dispute with another person.

turning into a monster

For only a few years are yet to come,
and I will walk a path that I cannot retrace,
my spirit ruined,   *17:1*
    my days dimmed—
        only graves for me.

I swear, I have to live with mocking,
    put up with their provocations
    even as I shut my eyes for sleep:
"Take my security!"—"There's my pledge!"—
    "Who will do business with me?"—
For You have really shut their minds from sense,
and that is why You will not let them rise.

"If one tells his thoughts to a flatterer,   *17:5*
the eyes of his sons will languish."
He displays me as a byword for nations,
    and I have turned to spittle in men's faces.
My eye has darkened with my troubles,
    my limbs all turned to shadow,
Men of goodwill are horrified at this,
    the innocent are roused against the flatterer,
while the righteous man holds to his course,
    and men of unsoiled hands increase resolve.

But you, all three, return!—Come back!—   *17:10*
Not one wise man do I find among you.
You turn the night to day,   *17:12*
    pretend that light is closer than the face of darkness.
My days have passed,   *17:11*

> my plans, my heartstrings
>> snapped.
> If I longed to make Sheol my home,
>> plump up my cushions in darkness,
> say to the pit, "You are my father,"
>> call the maggots "mother," "sister,"

17:15   where would be my hope?
>> Who could see any hope for me?
> Will it go down to the gates of Sheol?
>> Descend together with me to the dirt?

Ok Job is getting Dark here

Bildad's Second Speech

Bildad the Shuhite then took up the argument and said: 18:1

How long will you two keep speech at an end?
Think a while, but then let us speak!
Why are we acting like dumb animals?
   Why do you think we are blocked?

You who rip apart your own soul in your rage:
   Is the earth abandoned on your account,
   or the cliff dislodged from its place?
No: But the light of the wicked gutters,   18:5
   his hearth's flame does not glow;
      the light goes dark in his home,
         his lamp gutters in his hand.
His powerful stride is straitened,
      his own schemes overthrow him,
   for he has been sent off with nets at his feet;
      he walks on tangles,
catches his heel on snares.
      Traps hold him fast.
His noose is concealed in the ground,   18:10
      his snare on his path,
while terrors assail him from every side,
      strewn at his feet.
His strength wastes away in starvation,
   disaster stands at his side.

[handwritten annotation:] Job is being selfish, it is not the end of the world

Gobbled up are his sticks and skin;
    gobbled his sticks, by the Firstborn of Death.
He is ripped away from his tent, his trust,
    marched away to the King of Terror:
18:15   Now his tent dwells without him in it.
His home is seeded with sulfur:
    His roots dry up from beneath;
    above, his boughs wither.
All thought of him is lost to the earth,
    he has no fame in the countryside,
    driven from light to darkness
    banished from the world of men.
No child has he among his folk,
    no offspring;
    no trace of him where he once sojourned.

18:20   Latter-day men are shocked at his fate,
    just as the ancients were seized with horror:
    "These were once the abodes of the wicked;
    here lived the man who did not know El."

Job's Reply to Bildad's Second Speech

Job answered: *19:1*

How long will you keep on tormenting me,
   crushing me with words?
Ten times now, you have insulted me,
   treated me coldly, shamelessly.
But if I have really been at fault,
   does my fault wholly lie with me?
If you wish to act as my superiors   *19:5*
   and scold me for my own disgrace,
just know that a god behaving crookedly
   got his net around me.
So I cried, "Violence!" but got no answer,
   called for help but got no justice.
He hedged my path so I could not pass,
   threw darkness over all my lanes,
stripped me of my dignities,
   took away my crown.
He tore me down from every side till I was gone.   *19:10*
   He carried off my hope like so much lumber.
He fanned his rage against me,
   treated me like an enemy.
Together came his troops;
   they built their siege ramp up against me,
   camped around my tent.

abandonment

He made me alien to my very brothers;
    my friends are all estranged from me.
Relatives and intimates visit me no more,
19:15   my household folk neglect me.
My house girls take me for a stranger,
    see me as an outsider.
I called my servant. He would not answer—
    I had to beg him with my own mouth!
My breath is nauseating to my wife;
    my stench annoys my own children.
Even little ones find me revolting;
    I stand up, they make fun of me.
My former confidants despise me;
    people I loved have turned against me.
19:20 My bones cling to my skin and flesh,
    all I have left is the skin of my teeth.
Pity me, pity me, friends of mine,
    for the hand of a god has touched me.
Why do you persecute me like a god?
    Can't you get enough of my flesh?

self-importance

If only my story could be transcribed,
    if only it could be graven on copper
    with an iron stylus, or copied on lead,
    hewn into rock forever!
19:25 For I know my avenger lives somewhere,
    and he must someday come forward on earth,
    though this may be only after
    my skin has been hacked away.
But that I should see the god in my flesh,

see with my own eyes, no other's—
my whole being melts at the thought!

When you say, "Look how he is persecuted,"
    that the root of the matter must be in me—
fear the Sword—
yes, the Rage, the Sin-Sword—
that you may know Shaddai's doom.

Zophar's Second Speech

20:1   Zophar the Naamatite then took up the argument and said:

Dark thoughts of mine are spurring me to answer,
    on account of what I feel inside of me.
I hear reproaches meant to cause me shame,
    and an impulse from my mind bids me respond.

Are you aware that from the first,
    from the time that man was set upon earth,
20:5 the joy of the wicked is always brief,
    the bad man's pleasure lasts only an instant.
Though his stature rise to the heavens,
    though his head attain the clouds,
he meets the same end as his own stool;
    "Where has he gone?" the onlookers say.
He flies away like a dream,
    not to be found,
    wanders away like a night apparition.
The eye may have glimpsed him, but never again;
    his place will sight him no more.
20:10 His sons will have to placate the poor;
    their hands will restore what he gained by force,
while his bones, stuffed with his secret sin,
    lie rotting on the ground with him.

When evil sweetens in his mouth,
    he keeps it hidden under his tongue,

cherishes it, doesn't let it go,
holds it back beneath his palate.
But once in his entrails, that food turns bad,
turns to asp poison in his gut.

He swallowed wealth; now he pukes it up,   20:15
and God expels it from his belly.
He sucked asp venom;
the adder's tongue kills him.
He will not survive to see streams,
    rivers, torrents of honey and curd.

He restores the yield of his labors,
    he cannot absorb it.
"Like the wealth, the return"—
    no pleasure for him.
For he crushed, abandoned the poor,
    stole a house rather than build one.
For he never knew peace in his belly.   20:20
    His craving was such that he would let nothing escape.
    He ate until not a morsel remained,
        so how could he hope to be well?

Just when his measure is full, he feels pain,
    the whole hand of misery bears hard on him.
Just as he is filling his belly,
    the rage he's earned is loosed on him,
    rains down on him while he sits at his meat.
He flees the iron weapon;
    the bow's bronze pierces him through.
    Drawn, it comes out of his back—   20:25

a flash from his gallbladder brings down terror upon him.
All darkness is stored in his entrails;
  a flame unfanned burns him away—
  it will go ill with whatever is left in his tent.
The heavens uncover his sin,
  the earth rises against him,
  uncovers the bounty inside his house,
  flooding, flowing away on his doomsday.

This is what God has in store for the wicked;
  this, his lot from El.

Beware, Job.

Job's buddies are lying in the place of god. BAD

Job's Reply to Zophar's Second Speech

Job answered: 21:1

Listen carefully to what I have to say,
and let that be your act of consolation.
Bear with me and let me speak,
and mock me only when I have finished.
Is my complaint against a person?
How can I not be out of patience?
Look at me, take in the horror, 21:5
    hands in front of faces!
Just to think of it dismays me,
    shudders grip my body:
Why are the wicked allowed to live,
    grow old, and win prosperity,
their children with them, right before them,
    children's children before their eyes?
Their houses are secure from fear
    with no divine rod over them;
their bulls impregnate without fail, 21:10
    their cows drop calves without aborting;
they let their little ones frolic like sheep,
    their children dance,
    striking up the drum and lyre,
    gleeful at the sound of pipes.
They spend their days in luxury,
    and all at once—down to Sheol they go.

Yet they had said to El, "Away from us!
    We do not want to know Your ways.

21:15   Who is Shaddai that we should worship Him?
    What do we get out of praying to Him?"
Yet they could not have made their own prosperity.
(Incomprehensible to me, the thinking of the wicked!)
How often does the lamp of the bad man gutter,
    and due disaster fall on him?
Does God distribute pain-portions in His rage?
Do such men become straw before the wind,
    or storm-snatched chaff?

Does God store up the punishment for his sons?—
    He should requite the man himself, that he may know,

21:20   that his own eyes may witness his own doom,
    that he may drink the rage from Shaddai's venom bottle.
For what does he care about his family after him,
    once the number of his months has been determined?
Does he teach knowledge to God,
    who passes judgment on the mighty?
One man dies as well-off as can be,
    all at ease, contented,
    his breasts full of milk,
    his bones juicy with marrow;

21:25   another dies in bitterness,
    one who never had a taste of plenty:
They lie together in dirt
    blanketed by maggots.

Yes, I know exactly what you're thinking,
    your vicious malice toward me,

when you say,

    "What has become of the nobleman's house?

    Where are the tents where the wicked were dwelling?"

But haven't you questioned the travelers

    (for you cannot deny their signs)?—

The bad man is spared on the day of disaster,   *21:30*

    the day when acts of wrath are brought forth.

Who can reproach him to his face?

    He has acted: Who can requite him?

They bear him away to a sepulcher;

    he keeps watch over his mound;

        the riverbed clods are sweet in his mouth.

He draws all men after him;

    before him were men without number.

How, then, can you comfort me with nonsense?

    Your answers are simply betrayal.

You are supposed to be my friends

Eliphaz's Third Speech

22:1   Eliphaz the Temanite then took up the argument and said:

Is there anything a man can do for El?
    Can even a clever man do Him a favor?
Does Shaddai care if you are righteous,
    or does He profit if you perfect your ways?
Is He reproving you for piety?
    Is that why He is bringing you to judgment?

22:5   No!

Your evil is tremendous, your sins unending.

More and more convinced that Job is sinning

Just look:
You took your brothers' pledge for nothing,
    stripped the clothing from the naked,
gave the thirsty man no water,
    kept back bread from starving people.
Strong-arm men control the land,
    only those in favor live there.
You sent away widows empty-handed,
    left the arms of orphans crushed.

Wow. That is low.

22:10   That is why these snares surround you,
    sudden panic overwhelms you,
darkness too—you cannot see,
    blinded by a flood of waters.

After all:
God is in the heights of heaven—

look how high are the topmost stars—
so you have said, "What can God know?

No one will see

How can He judge from behind the clouds?
Clouds seclude Him—can He see,
   as He strolls around the heavens' rim?"

Indeed: 22:15
You are true to the ancient way
trodden by sinful men of old,
men destroyed before time was,
their foundation swept into the flood,
who said to El, "Away from us!"
   What could Shaddai do for them?
Yet He had filled their houses with plenty!
   (Incomprehensible to me, the thinking of the wicked!)
The righteous looked on, delighted,
   the guiltless mocked them:
"Just look! Our substance remains intact;   22:20
   but their wealth is consumed by fire."

Get close to Him and live securely—
   all good things will come to you.
Take instruction from His mouth;
   set His commands inside your heart.
Return to Shaddai and you will increase;
   rid your tent of criminal goods—
you will find ore in the very dirt,
   Ophir-gold in rock-born streams.

That's what I've been doing my whole life?

   You will have ore in god-size masses,   22:25
   hills of silver will be yours.
Then you will take pleasure in Shaddai,

lift your face up to the god,
enjoy His favor.
When you call Him, He will hear you;
then you will fulfill your vows.
Decree your bidding—it is done!
Light will shine upon your paths.
When others are low, you will say, "Rise up!"
for He saves those whose eyes are low.

22:30   He will save the guiltless man—
save him thanks to your own pure palms.

Job's Reply to Eliphaz's Third Speech

Job answered: 23:1

Again today, my complaint is bitter:
    Heavier than my groan
    is the hand that weighs me down.

If only I knew how to find Him,
    if only I could reach His seat,
lay out my case before Him,
    and fill my mouth with arguments,

[margin note: court]

then I would learn what words He'd find to answer,   23:5
    and could consider what He'd say to me.
Would He use force, disputing with me?
    Oh no!—He would pay me close attention.
For there, good men contend with Him;
    there I could save myself forever from my judge.

But no: Forward I go, but He is gone,
    backward, and I cannot perceive Him.
He makes for the left—I cannot make Him out;
    twists to the right, and I cannot see.

[margin note: He has abandoned me]

If He knew my ways, if He would test me,   23:10
    I would emerge like gold,
      for my foot has kept to His footprints;
        I held to His way, not swerving,

never failed the bidding of His lips,
  treasured the words of His mouth more than my daily
    bread.
But He is single-minded—who can deter Him?
  He does whatever His heart desires.
When He exhausts what is allotted me,
  He has more of the same in store;

23:15 that is why I panic in His presence—
  just the thought of Him makes me shake.
Yes, El has turned my spirit feeble,
  Shaddai has thrown me into panic,
for the dark has not yet cut me off;
  death's gloom has not yet covered up my face.

24:1 Why are certain times not set aside by Shaddai?
  Why can His familiars not anticipate His days?

They push back boundary markers,
  make off with flocks and tend them,
  lead away the orphan's donkey,
  take in pawn the widow's ox,
  shove the paupers off the road;
  poor country folk all have to hide.

24:5   They live in the steppe like wild asses,
      go out to their labor at dawn
      to seek what will sustain them.
    To them, the desert means bread for the young.
    In the fields they harvest his fodder,
    glean the wicked man's vineyards.
    They pass the night naked, uncovered,
    unprotected from the cold,

drenched by the streams running off the mountains,
    clinging to a cliff for want of shelter.
They steal the orphan from the breast,
  take pledges from the poor,
    who go about naked, uncovered,   24:10
    craving food as they carry the sheaves;
    who press out oil within rich men's walls,
    tread wine into vats, though thirsty themselves.
In the town, they die groaning—
  the cut throats of corpses still screaming.
    The god attaches no blame.

Here are some of those who defy the light,
  who do not know its ways
  or dwell in its paths:
The murderer rises at evening   24:14a
  to kill the destitute beggar.
The adulterer's eye longs for twilight,   24:15
  saying, "No eye will see me";
  he makes it a mask for his face.
At night, along comes the sneak thief,   24:14b,16
  burrowing into houses in darkness.
They seal themselves up indoors by day,
  know not the light.
For all of them, morning is deathdark;
  but deathdark's horror they know quite well.
By day they flee lightly over the waters,
  avoiding their cursed plot of land,
  not turning in to the vineyards,
  lest they be sighted by men.

As desert and heat melt the snow gently,
  steal it away so that no trace remains,
  so they sin and die without suffering,
  vanish not leaving a trace.
24:20 His lovers forget him, the worm finds him tasty,
  his name is forgotten;
  the guilty man cracks like a tree.
He crushes the barren for not bearing,
  bitter though she herself may be;
  he crushes the widow who has no protector.
He draws mighty men with his power and kills them:
  Rising, they feel insecure for their lives,
  they bribe him for their security, trusting;
  he watches their steps,
  and looks for the chance to pursue them.
  They flee a short way—he leaves town on their heels,
  and like everyone else, they are crushed too.
  He stops up their mouths, their cries are not heard.
  They wither at once,
  like the topmost ear of the standing corn.
24:25 Is all this not true? Who will call me a liar?
Who can refute the words I have spoken?

Bildad's Third Speech

Bildad the Shuhite took up the argument and said: 25:1

Dominion and terror belong to Him,
   to Him who makes peace in His lofty places.
Can anyone number His troops?
   On whom does His light not rise?

How can man be innocent with El?
   How can woman's brood be pure?—   25:5
Even the moon does not gleam bright,
   even the stars are not pure in His eyes.
What then, maggot-man, earth's worm-child?

[handwritten annotations:] No one is innocent

[handwritten:] BURN!. BoomRoasted!.

Job's Reply to Bildad's Third Speech

26:1   Job answered:

What help your impotence offers!
    What support from your unmighty arm!
Such advice, from one with no wisdom!
    What clever ideas you propose!
To whom are you speaking such words?
    Whose breath is that passing through you?

26:5   Shades quail
    beneath the waters and their inhabitants.
Sheol confronts Him naked,
    Abaddon uncovered.
He stretched Mount Zaphon over chaos,
    suspended the earth above the void,
bound up the waters into clouds
    (yet the clouds never burst beneath them),
covered the face of the Throne,
    blanketed it with His cloud,
26:10   scribed a circle on the water's surface,
    to mark the limits of light and darkness.
Heaven's pillars quaked, shocked at His rebuke.
With His might, He quelled Yamm-ocean;
    smashed Rahab with His cunning.
With His wind, He got Yamm-ocean in a net,
    His hand pierced the Elusive Serpent.

Sarcasm

These are but a few of His exploits,
vague rumors we have heard of Him.
But who could gaze at Him when He thunders in might?

What does this mean?
God is mighty? Who can stand
up for themselves when they
feel wronged by him. We
are too trivial?

Job's Last Word to His Friends

27:1   Job went on with his poem:

Now I take my solemn oath:
By the life of El who denies me justice,
    by Shaddai who has turned my soul to gall:
As long as I have breath in me,
    while the god is breathing life into my nostrils,
never will my lips speak evil,
    or my tongue pronounce a falsehood.
27:5   Never will I call you right,
        never deny my innocence
        until the day I die!
I insist I am right, I will not yield.
    My heart will not be cause for blame
        however long I live.

May my enemy be like the wicked;
    my opponent like the scoundrel.
For what hope has the villain from his gains
    when God makes him self-satisfied?
Will God listen to his cry
    when he finds himself in trouble?
27:10   Will he have satisfaction from Shaddai
        though he call and call upon Him?
Let me teach you the power of God,
    and not conceal Shaddai's designs.

(But you have all seen this for yourselves,
    so how can your speech be so vapid?) *empty*

Here is what God has in store for the wicked,
    the tyrant's lot that he gets from Shaddai: *What God does to the wkd*

He raises children for the sword,
    his heirs will always lack bread.

His survivors are buried by plague,
    unmourned by his widows.   *27:15*

He may heap up silver like dirt,
    and lay up fine garments like heaps of clay— *others will own it*

he may lay them up, but the righteous will wear them,
    guiltless men will share out his silver.

He builds his house like the moth's,
    like a lean-to some watchman made.

He lies down, a rich man,
but before he is settled,
    opens his eyes—nothing is left.

Terror overtakes him like a torrent;   *27:20*
at night, the storm snatches him away;
the East Wind seizes him and he vanishes—
    hurls him, whirls him away from his place,
        throws him down somewhere, pitiless—
how he would love to flee from its grip!
    It slaps-claps its hands, jeering at him,
hisses at him in his new place.

A wicked man may be rich, but it will all be taken away

A Meditation on Wisdom

28:1 We know there is a place where gold is found,
         and somewhere there is silver for refining.
      Iron is extracted out of earth,
         and copper out of solid rock.
      He puts an end to darkness,
         delves to every uttermost limit
            in quest of stones of gloom and deathdark,
      bursts a channel from his dwelling
      to places footfall-forgotten,
         folk-thinned, wandered from;
28:5 a land no longer yielding bread,
         gone to rubble, as if by fire,
            but where the stones are sapphires,
               and the dirt, gold;
      a path the vulture does not know,
         never scanned by the falcon's eye,
      never trodden by proud wild beasts,
         never crossed by serpents.
      He seizes the flint with his own bare hands,
         overturns mountains by the root,
28:10 splits channels wide as Niles through bedrock;
         takes in with his eye every item of value.
      He dams the rivers' nether sources
         to bring their mysteries to light.

      But wisdom—where can it be found?
      Where is the place of true knowledge?

No man knows how to reach it,
for it is not found in the land of the living.
 Abyss declares, "It is not in me!"
 Ocean echoes, "Nor is it here!"
You cannot buy it for solid gold,   28:15
 its price cannot be weighed out in silver.
It cannot be valued in gold from Ophir,
 in precious onyx or sapphire.
It has no match in gold or glass,
 cannot be traded for golden trinkets,
  not even to mention corals or crystal!
Wisdom is better than bags of rubies;
 it has no match in the topaz of Kush,
 cannot be valued in purest gold.

Where is the source of wisdom, then?   28:20
 Where is the place of true knowledge?
It is hidden away from the eyes of the living,
 even concealed from birds of the sky.
Abaddon and Mot declare,
"We know of it only by rumor!"

God perceives its path.
 He knows its place.

Peering out to the ends of the earth,
inspecting everything under the heavens,
to weigh out the winds,
 apportion the water,
  set quotas of rain,
   fix routes for the thundershowers,   28:25

He saw it, appraised it,
examined it and plumbed it,
and then He said to man:
    "The fear of the Lord is wisdom;
    true knowledge is avoiding sin."

God will keep the machine of
earth running as long as
Man follows the Lord and
avoids sin.

BUT → He will give you
free will to do as you

please.

Job Reviews His Condition Past and Present

Job went on with his poem: 29:1

If only I could be under the moons of old again,
back in the days when the god watched over me!
When He held His lamp so it shone above my head,
and I could walk by the light in darkness.
If I could be again as I was in my daring days,
with the god above my tent, protecting;
when Shaddai was still with me— 29:5

    my men around me too!—
my feet washed with butter,
    the rocks pouring oil out for me in streams!

When I would stride out to the gate of the town,
    and take my place in the city square,
young men would see me and hide in the crowd,
    elders would rise and stand still in their places;
chieftains would dam their words' flow,
    putting their hands to their lips;
commanders' voices were muffled; 29:10
    tongues stuck to the roofs of mouths;
but ears would hear and admire;
    eyes would see and bear witness to me:
how I rescued poor men when they cried,
    and orphans, people none would help.

Desperate, ruined men would bless me,
    and I brought song to the widow's heart.
I put on justice and it suited me;
    my decree was my turban and robe.

29:15   I was the blind man's eyes;
I was feet for the lame;
I was father to the poor.
I studied the stranger's complaint.
I cracked the fangs of villains,
    ripped the prey from their teeth.
So I said:
I will die in my nest,
    live as long as the phoenix,
my roots open to water,
    my shoots night-moistened by dew.

29:20   My pride constantly renewed for me,
    my bow blooming in my hand. . . .

They would listen to me, waiting
silently for my advice;
when I had spoken they would not ask again,
once my word had dripped over them.
They would look to me as if for rain,
    their mouths wide to the spring showers.
When I smiled at them, they were uneasy;
    they took care not to make my face fall.

29:25   I chose their paths;
I sat at their head;
I dwelt among them like a king with his troops,
    or like one who comforts men who mourn.

And now I find myself mocked by men younger than myself,   *30:1*
men whose fathers I rejected from working alongside my
sheepdogs!

Even their manual labor, what good was it to me?
Their vigor was long gone
in dearth and famine, barren,
fleeing to the wilderness,
a horror-night of ruin;
plucking saltwort from scrub-brush,
burning broom-root to get warm,
driven from society,   *30:5*
shouted at like thieves;
squatting in the wadi-channels,
dust-caves, cliff-hollows;
braying in the bushes,
keeping company among thorns;
louts' brood, no one's children,
ousted from the world of men—
now I am their mocking song,
the topic of their gossip!
They scorn me, they shun me,   *30:10*
they spare my face no spit.

For He undid my cord, tormented me,
and they shake loose my reins.
Young bullies crop up on my right,
range anywhere they like,
pave right up to me their highways of destruction,

ruin my own paths.
They work effectively to bring me down,
 they need no help.
They come on like a wide rush of water,
 downward, ravaging, rolling.

You cannot handle the betrayal

30:15   Horror has rolled over me,
and driven off my dignity like wind;
my wealth has vanished like a cloud,
and now my life is spilling out of me.
Days of suffering have seized me;
 by night my bones are hacked from me,
 my sinews cannot rest.
Just to dress takes all my strength;
my collar fits my waist.

destitute + starving

He conceived me as clay,
and I have come to be like dust and ashes.

The Machine / diagrams

30:20   I cry to You—no answer;
 I stand—You stare at me,
You harden Yourself to me,
 spurn me with Your mighty hand.
You lift me up and mount me on a wind,
 dissolve my cunning,
and I know that You will send me back to death,
 to the house awaiting every living creature.
But why this violence to a pile of rubble?
 In his disaster is there some salvation?
30:25   Did I not weep for the hapless?

Did my soul not grieve for the poor?
Yes—
I hoped for good, got only wrong;
   I hoped for light, got only darkness.
My insides seethe and never stop,
   I face days of suffering,
I go about in sunless gloom.
In assembly I stand up and wail,
changed to a jackal's brother,
   fellow to the ostrich.
My skin has blackened on my body,   *30:30*
   my bones are charred with fever.
My lyre has gone to mourning,
   my pipe to the sound of sobs.

Job's Oath

31:2   Then what does the god above have in store,
       what lot from Shaddai in the heavens?
Only disaster for doers of evil,
       estrangement for men who do wrong.
Does He not see my ways,
       count all my steps?

31:5   Have I walked the way of falsehood?
       Was my foot fleet to deceit?
Let God weigh me in an honest balance—
       He will have to see my innocence.

If my step has left the path,
if my heart has obeyed my eye,
if anyone's goods have stuck to my palms,
       may I sow for another to eat;
       may my offspring be uprooted.
If I have let a woman beguile me,
if I have lurked at my neighbor's door,

31:10   may my own wife grind for another,
       may other men crouch over her;
       for that would be indecent, foul,
       that would be a crime for the judges.
       For it is fire
       raging down to Abaddon
       and would uproot my increase.

31:1   I have made a pact with my eyes

never to gaze at young women.
If I deny my men-slaves or women-slaves justice
when they raise complaints to me,
    what will I do when God comes forward,
    to demand accounting?
    What will I answer Him?
    Did not my maker make him in the selfsame belly,   31:15
    form us in a single womb?
If I have refused the poor their wants,
    or made the eyes of widows languish,
if I have eaten my bread alone,
without an orphan sharing it
    (for since I was a boy, I raised him like a father,
    and from my mother's womb I guided her)—
If ever I saw someone dying naked,
or a poor man with no clothing,
    I swear, his very loins would bless me,   31:20
    as he warmed himself in the wool of my sheep.
If ever I raised my hand to an orphan,
seeing I had support in the gate,
    may my shoulder fall out of its socket,
    and my forearm break off at the elbow;
    for disaster from El is terror to me;
    I cannot bear His awesome looming.
If ever I put my hope in gold,
    or thought to place my trust in it;
if I was smug because my wealth was great,   31:25
    because my hand had acquired so much—
If I have ever looked at the sun as it beamed,
or at the moon coming on in splendor,

and my heart was secretly beguiled,
and my hand crept up to touch my mouth,
    that too would be a crime for judges,
     for it would mean denying God on high.
If ever I rejoiced in my enemy's downfall,
or felt a rush of joy when trouble found him,
31:30   never did I let my mouth taste sin,
    asking for his life by execration.
If the men of my household ever failed to say,
"Why did we consume his flesh?"—
    No stranger ever spent the night in the street;
    for I would open my doors to the wanderer.
If, as men will, I hid my crimes,
    concealed my sin inside me,
    fearing public scandal,
    frightened by the scorn of clans,
    kept silent, never setting foot outdoors—
If my land cries out because of me,
    and its furrows weep together,
31:39   if I consumed its produce without paying,
    made its workers sigh their souls out,
31:40a may it sprout up thorns instead of wheat,
    stinkweed instead of barley.

31:35   If only I had someone to hear me!

    Here is my desire: that Shaddai answer me,
    that my opponent write a brief;
31:36   I swear that I would wear it on my shoulder,
    bind it on me like a crown.

I would tell my steps to Him by number,   *31:37*
    come before Him as before a prince.

Here Job's speeches ended.   *31:40b*

Elihu Speaks

32:1 Then these three men stopped discoursing with Job, because
he was right in his own eyes. But Elihu ben Barakhel the
Buzite of the clan of Ram became angry at Job, very angry,
for thinking himself, rather than God, to be in the right. He
was angry, too, at his three friends for not finding an
answer, and thereby making God appear to be in the wrong.
Elihu waited to speak with Job, for they were years older than
32:5 he. When Elihu saw that the three men had no more to say,
he became angry.

Elihu ben Barakhel the Buzite took up the argument and
said:

I am younger by years, and you are elderly,
so I shrank, afraid
to speak my mind before you.
I said to myself that days would speak,
    that length of years would utter wisdom,
but it seems that man needs inspiration—
    Shaddai's breath—to lend him understanding.
Elders are not always wise,
    the venerable may lack judgment,
32:10 so I ask you for a hearing,
    let me also speak my mind.
I waited patiently while you spoke,
    attended to your wisdom while you tried out words.

[handwritten marginalia:] and disbelief
[handwritten marginalia:] but maybe only from anger
[handwritten marginalia:] Break from traditional thought

I paid you close attention,
but I see that no one has refuted Job,
  or made rebuttal to his speeches.
Do not say, "Now we have met true wisdom!
  A god is refuting us, not a man!"
Had he matched words with me,
  I would have answered him—
  but not with words like yours.

Intimidated, they stopped arguing;   *32:15*
  words abandoned them.
I waited for them to stop speaking,
  and now that they are still and argue no more,
I too shall speak my piece;
  let me too speak my mind.
For I am overfull with words,
  strained by the wind in my belly.
My belly is like unopened wine,
  like new wineskins about to split;
let me speak and get relief,   *32:20*
  open my lips and make response.
I shall not be partial to any man,
  or soften my words for anyone.
Indeed, if I knew how to soften my words,
  my maker would soon carry me off.

But listen, Job, to what I have to say,   *33:1*
  pay heed to all my words.
You see me opening my mouth to speak,
  my tongue against my palate:

My speeches are my heart's own truth;
   my lips speak wisdom in plain words.
El's spirit has made me what I am,
   and Shaddai's breath has quickened me.
33:5 If you are able, answer me;
   get into place and brace yourself!
I am no better than you before God;
   I was pinched from clay, like you.
Terror of me will not cow you,
   and no compulsion from me will weigh you down.
But in my hearing you have said,
   and I have caught your words:
"I am pure and guiltless,
   I am innocent and I have done no wrong,
33:10   but He invents pretexts for anger,
      regards me as His enemy.
   He puts my feet in stocks,
     monitors my every step."
Now here you are not right, I tell you,
   for God is greater than any man.
Why have you complained to Him
   that He does not answer all man's words?
For El speaks once,
   and El speaks twice,
   yet man is not aware!
33:15 In a dream, in a vision of night,
   when slumber drifts down upon men
   as they drowse upon their beds—
that is when He opens the ears of men,
   and frightens them with due correction,

Knowledge

deterring a man from evil deeds,
    and smothering a person's pride,
saving his life from the Pit,
    and his spirit from passing the Death Canal.
He is chastened with pain while still on his bed;
    unending bone-trembling.
His appetite turns against his food,   33:20
    delicacies turn his stomach.
His flesh wastes away—he can hardly be seen—
    his bones are abraded to invisibility.
His life approaches the brink of the Pit,
    it nearly belongs to the Killers—
but if there is just a single angel,
    one advocate among a thousand
to speak for that man's character,
    to pity him and say,
"Spare him from descending to the Pit!
    I have found ransom,"
his flesh becomes fleshier than in youth,   33:25
    returns to his boyhood vigor.
He appeals to a god and finds approval,
    enters his presence with shouts of joy
    (for man is repaid for his righteousness).
He beams at his fellow men and declares,
    "I sinned, perverted what is right,
    and it availed me nothing.
He redeemed my life and saved me from the Pit,
    and I survived to enjoy the light."
All these things the god will do
    two or three times for a man,

33:30   sending him back from the edge of the Pit,
      lighting him back to the land of the living.

Listen, Job, and pay attention,
    be quiet, let me speak.
If you have arguments, answer me;
    speak, for I want to put you right.
But if you do not, then hear me out
    in silence, while I teach you wisdom.

Elihu's Second Speech

Elihu took up the argument and said: *34:1*

Hear my words, you sages!
   Men of learning, pay attention.
The ear is the best judge of speech,
   the palate knows what food is tasty,
so let us make our own determination,
   discover what is right among ourselves.
Now Job has stated, "I am righteous,   *34:5*
   but the god denies me justice.
   I declare my verdict false,
   a deadly arrow for a guiltless man."
Is there any man like Job,
   who drinks derision like water,
who keeps the company of wicked men,
   and walks with malefactors,
who says, "There is no benefit for man
   in pleasing God"?
Listen, therefore, men of reason: *34:10*
   Sacrilege, to say that El does evil,
   or that Shaddai does wrong.
Rather, He repays a man for what he's done,
   provides for him according to his conduct.
In fact, God never does do wrong,
   Shaddai is not corrupt in judgment.
Who put the world into His charge?
   Who set up all creation?

34:15
If He should set His mind to taking back
   the breath of life, the spirit that is His,
all creatures made of flesh would die together,
   and man return to the ground.

If it is understanding that you seek, hear this;
   listen to my resounding words.
Can one who has contempt for justice govern?
   Will you declare the Righteous Master evil?
Does one call the king a scoundrel,
   or the nobles, wicked?—
a king who never favored princes,
   never put the rich before the poor,
   for all are the works of His hand.

34:20
They die with no warning, at midnight;
   whole nations go into upheaval and vanish,
   great men disappear, as if by no hand.
For His eyes are on a man's behavior;
   He sees his every step.
There is no place so dark,
   that wicked men can hide there,
   not even the obscurity of death.
For El does not set man a certain date
   to come before Him to be judged.
He shatters the mighty, more than can be numbered,
   replaces them with others.

34:25
Indeed, He finds out everything they've done,
   overturns them overnight, and they are ruined.
He strikes them down among the criminals,
   where everyone can see,

because they turned away from Him,
   and never learned His ways,
    bringing the cry of needy men to Him
    who heeds the poor man's cry.
If He should choose to hold His peace,
    who could condemn Him?
   If He should hide His face, who could behold Him,
    be it man or nation?
Better this than for the impious to rule,   *34:30*
   better this than snares for people.

For has he said to God, "Now I have borne
   the punishment and I will do no further harm.
   Show me Yourself the things I have not seen,
   and if I have done wrong, I will no more"?
Should He repay you on the terms you set yourself?
Is that why you reject His judgment?
You decide, not I!
Just speak, and tell us what you know.

Reasonable men will say to me,
   as any wise man would
   who may have overheard me,
"Job is not speaking from wisdom;   *34:35*
   his speeches make no sense."
I would love to see Job tested to the limit,
   for he argues like the wicked,
    then compounds his sin with treason,
    when he slaps his hands among us,
    and delivers long harangues concerning God.

Elihu's Third Speech

35:1 Elihu took up the argument and said:

Is this your idea of good judgment—
    to say, "I am more righteous than God"?
You ask what good it does you,
    what do you gain by not sinning.
I will answer you with words,
    you and your friends beside you.

35:5 Look up at the heavens and see,
    behold the clouds, so much higher than you:
If you do sin, can it affect Him?
    If you do much wrong, how does it touch Him?
If you are righteous, what have you given Him?
    What can He gain from your hand?
Your wrongs come back to your own kind,
    your goodness redounds to men like you.

Downtrodden masses are wailing,
    crying out under the strong man's arm.
35:10 No one inquires, "Where is God, our maker,
    who grants us song by night,
    who makes us wiser than the land-bound beasts,
    more far-seeing than the birds of heaven?"
There they cry out
    because of the pride of the wicked,

and He does not answer;
but it is false that El is deaf,
   or that Shaddai does not observe;
and if you say that you do not see Him—
   lay your case before Him,
      then wait for Him.

But now, since he has chosen otherwise,   35:15
   his rage controls him,
   and he is utterly devoid of peace of mind.
Clearly, Job's mouth utters nonsense,
   haughty words in ignorance spoken.

Elihu's Fourth Speech

36:1 Elihu went on and said:

Have a moment's patience while I speak,
for yet there is a word or two
to say in the god's behalf.

No! Don't speak for God

I will make my thoughts heard far and wide,
as I proclaim my maker just,
for truly, none of my words is false;
a man of sound opinion stands before you.

36:5 Behold! Mighty El does not reject a man for nothing;
mighty, His heart's power.
He does not let the wicked live,
does justice to the poor.
He does not take His eye away from righteous men;
sets them high on thrones with kings,
in everlasting elevation.
But when it comes to people bound in chains,
or caught up in the noose of poverty,
He tells them what they've done,
and lists their deeds,
when their crimes have overcome them.

36:10 He opens their ear to reproach,
and tells them to repent their sin.
If they obey and serve Him,
they finish out their days in bounty,

end their years in luxury.
But if they refuse,
    they cross beyond the Death Canal
    and die unwitting.
Men of evil spirit harbor rage;
    do not cry out when He has bound them;
they die still young,
    live out their lives among the holy shades.
He releases the sufferer through suffering,
    opens His ears through hardship.   36:15
Take you:
He turned you from the brink of trouble,
    set you in an open space,
        unstraitened place,
    laid succulent food upon your table,
while *you* upheld the justice of the wicked,
    the justice and the judgment they rely on.
This rage now is designed to turn you from riches,
    from letting great bribes divert you.
Will your wealth carry weight with Him when you are in trouble,
    that, or any effort of strength?
Do not long for the night, when whole nations vanish abruptly.
Beware, do not turn to sin;   36:20
    choose poverty rather than that!

Behold! El, sublime in power;
    who equals Him as a master?
Who orders Him to act as He does,
    or says to Him, "You have done wrong"?
Remember to proclaim His works sublime,

His works at which all mankind gazes,

36:25   and every person contemplates,

       mankind, peering from afar.

Behold! El, sublime beyond our knowing,

    His years beyond all numbering.

He reserves the drops of water,

    refines the rain for fog,

    so that the clouds can drip,

    pour down on multitudes of people.

But who can grasp the unfurling of the clouds

    amid the thunderclaps from His pavilion?

36:30   Behold! He spreads His lightning over the clouds,

    blankets the roots of the sea;

with them He dooms some nations,

    grants abundant food to others.

He fills His palms with lightning,

    directs it with sure aim.

His thunder speaks of it—

    of His furious rage against evil—

37:1   this too makes my heart take fright

    and leap out of its place.

Listen! Listen! The rage in His voice!

    The rumbling from His mouth emerging!

He lets it loose under the whole heaven,

    its flash to the ends of the earth;

    and then, the voice roars.

He thunders in His majestic voice,

    but once the voice has sounded,

    no one can trace its path.

37:5   El thunders with His voice uncanny,

who makes things great beyond our knowing.
For to the snow He says, "Fall earthward!"
    Likewise, the rain, the downpour—
        the rain of His mighty downpour.
He seals up every man indoors,
    so that all will know His works.
The wild beasts retreat to their lairs,
    and settle down inside their dens.
Then from its chamber comes the storm,
    from the scatter-wind, the cold:
The breath of El makes ice set,   *37:10*
    the wide water solid.
But then He drives off, clears the storm-cloud;
    now the puff-cloud scatters light.
And so He alternates with twists and cunning changes,
    so that they do whatever He commands them
    downward to the surface of the earth:
But whether for the rod, sufficiency, or grace,
    He is the source.
Pay attention, Job, to this:
    Stop and think about El's wonders.
Can you tell when the god will alight on them,   *37:15*
    light the cloud up with His gleam?
Can you grasp, in the cloud's unfurlings,
    the wonders of His perfect knowledge,
you who find your clothing stifling,
    when the South Wind silences the earth?
Do you pound out the heavens by His side,
    turn them solid as a brazen mirror?
Tell us what we are to say of Him;

we cannot argue in this darkness!

37:20   If I do speak, will His tale be told?

Whatever mortals say just covers Him up the more!

And now, His lightning is no longer seen,

but brightness fills the skies,

for a breeze as it passed has made them glow,

a breeze from the north, the source of gold,

where the god abides in dreadful majesty.

Shaddai: We cannot find Him out—

sublime in power and judgment;

great master of justice.

He will never answer.

Therefore, mortals, fear Him

whom even men of wisdom cannot see.

Yahweh's Reply to Job

Yahweh answered Job from the storm:

Who dares speak darkly words with no sense?

Cinch your waist like a fighter.
I will put questions, and you will inform me:
Where were you when I founded the earth?
Speak, if you have any wisdom:
Who set its measurements, if you know,
    laid out the building lot, stretching the plumb line?
Where was the ground where He sank its foundations?
Who was setting the cornerstone
when the morning stars were all singing,
    when the gods were all shouting, triumphant?
Who barred the sea behind double gates
as it was gushing out of the womb?
When I made the clouds its covering, fog its swaddling,
broke its will with my decree,
set bar and double gate,
and said, "This far, no farther!
    Here stops your breakers' surge."
When did you ever give dawn his orders,
    assign the rising sun his post,
to grasp the corners of the world
    and shake the wicked out of it,
make the world heave, break like a seal of clay:
    They stand up naked.

38:15 The wicked are denied their light,
    the haughty arm is broken.

Have you ever reached the depths of the sea
    and walked around there, exploring the abyss?
Have you been shown behind the Gates of Death,
    or seen the Gates of Deathdark?
Have you beheld the earth's expanses?
Tell me, if you know everything!—
Where is the path to where light dwells,
    and darkness, where does it belong?
38:20 Can you conduct them to their regions,
    or even imagine their homeward paths?
You must know, you were born long ago!
    So many years you have counted!

Have you reached the stores of snow,
    or seen the stock of hailstones
that I have laid up for times of trouble,
    days of battle, days of war?

Where is the path to where lightning forks,
    when an east wind scatters it over the ground?
38:25 Who cracked open a channel for the torrent,
    clove the path for the thundershower,
to rain on lands where no man lives,
    on wildernesses uninhabited,
to feed a wasteland, fill a desolation,
    make it flower, sprout grass?
Does the shower have a father?

Who begot the drops of dew?
From whose womb did the ice come forth?
Who gave birth to the sky-frost—
   water clotting as to stone,   38:30
      the abyss congeals.

Do you tie the Sky-Sisters with ropes
   or undo Orion's bonds?
Do you bring out the stars as they are due,
   guide the Great Bear and her young?
Do you know the laws that rule the sky,
   and can you make it control the earth?
Can you thunder at the clouds
   so that a flood of water covers you?
Can you loose the lightning,   38:35
   and have it say, as it goes, "Your servant!"?
Who gave wisdom to the ibis,
   gave the cock its knowledge?
Who is wise enough to count the clouds,
   pour out the jars of heaven,
when the soil is fused solid
   and clods stick thickly?

Do you hunt prey for the lioness?
   Do you satisfy her young,
when they are crouching in their lair,   38:40
   sitting in ambush in the covert?
Who puts prey in the raven's way,
   when her fledglings cry to God,
      wandering, aimless, without food?

39:1   Do you know when the antelope gives birth,
        watch for the calving of the deer?
    Do you count the months they have to pass,
        know how, when their time has come,
        they crouch, split open for their young,
        release their newborns?
    The calves thrive, grow in the wild,
        then leave them, never return.

39:5   Who gave the wild ass his freedom,
        undid his bonds—
    the beast I made to live in wasteland,
        gave the salt flat as a home,
    so that he might laugh at crowded cities
        and never hear the driver's call,
    but scour the hills for pasturage,
        hunting for any bit of green?

    Does the buffalo deign to serve you?
        Will he sleep by your feeding trough?
39:10   Can you tie him to a furrow with a rope?
        Will he harrow the plain behind you?
    Can you rely on him, for all his power,
        and leave your work to him?
    Can you trust him to bring in your produce
        and heap it up for threshing?

    Delightful is the ostrich wing—
        but is it a pinion, like stork or vulture?

She leaves her eggs on the ground,
　　warms them in the sand,
forgets that they could be crushed by feet,　　　　　　　39:15
　　trampled by beasts.
Hard to her young—they might be anyone's.
　　Her labor for nothing?—no fear!
Yes, God deprived her of wisdom,
　　created her without sense;
yet when she runs up a hill
　　she can laugh at stallion and rider!

Do you give the stallion his strength?
　　Do you clothe his neck in a fearsome mane?
Do you make him thunder like a locust swarm?　　　　39:20
　　His awesome snort is terror.
With his hooves he strikes holes in the ground;
　　thrilled with his own force,
　　he advances to battle.
He laughs, dauntless, at fear,
　　never turns back in the face of the sword.
Around him quivers rattle,
　　lances and javelins flash,
but he gulps ground, raging and roiling;
　　cannot stand still when the battle horn sounds.
The battle horn sounds! "Hooray!" he cries.　　　　　39:25
He can smell a battle from afar,
　　thunder of fighters, charge-cries.

Does the vulture take wing from your wisdom,
　　when he spreads his pinions southward?

Does the eagle soar at your bidding,
    building his nest up high?—
He dwells, shelters on cliffs,
    on rock crags and fastnesses.

39:30   From there he seeks food,
    and his eyes peer far;
    his chicks lap gore.
Where there's a corpse you will find him.

Yahweh turned back to Job: 40:1

One who brings Shaddai to court should fight!
   He who charges a god should speak.

But Job answered Yahweh:

I see how little I am.
I will not answer You.
I am putting my hand to my lips:
   One time I spoke;   40:5
      I will not speak again;
   two times I spoke,
      and I will not go on.

Thank God, I get that I am a tiny pixel of the picture

40:6   Yahweh answered Job from the storm:

Cinch your waist like a fighter.
    I will put questions, and you will inform me.
Would you really annul my judgment,
    make me out to be guilty, and put yourself in the right?
Is your arm as mighty as God's?
    Does your voice thunder like His?

40:10   Just dress up in majesty, greatness!
    Try wearing splendor and glory!
Snort rage in every direction!
    Seek out the proud, bring him down!
Seek out the proud man, subdue him,
    crush cruel men where they stand,
hide them together in dirt,
    bind them in the Hidden Place:
Then even I would concede to you,
    when your right hand had gained you a triumph.

40:15   Just look at the River Beast that I put alongside you:
He eats grass like cattle.
Look at his thighs: What power!
    The might in his belly muscles!
He wills his tail into cedar—
    his thigh-thews twist tight.
His bones are unyielding bronze,

his limbs are like iron bars.
He is the first of God's ways.
   Let none but his maker bring forth his sword!

   For the hills bring their yield, their tribute to him,   *40:20*
   the hills where the wild beasts play—
to him, who lies under the lotus,
in a marsh, in a covert of reeds.

Sheltered, shaded by lotus,
surrounded by droop-leaf willows.
Look: He gulps a whole river, but languidly,
calm, as the Jordan surges into his mouth!

   Can you catch him by the eye?
   Can you pierce his nose with thorns?

Can you draw the River Coiler with a hook?   *40:25*
   Bind down his tongue with a rope?
String him through the nose with a reed?
   Bore his cheek with a thistle?
Would he beg you for mercy,
   gentle you with words?
Would he deign to be your ally?
   Could you make him a slave for life?
Could you pet him like a bird,
   leash him for your girls to play with?
Will partners haggle over him   *40:30*
   or cut him into lots for mongers?

Can you fill his skin with darts,
    get his head into a fishnet?
Just put your hand on him—
you will remember the battle, you will not do it again!

41:1   Look: Hope of him is delusion;
        even to glance at him is to fall.
           Is he not fierce when aroused?
    Who could stand ground in his presence?
        Who could address him unscathed?
    Under all the heavens, that man would be mine!
        I would not silence his boasting,
        his talk of feats,
           his grace in battle.

41:5   Who could strip away the surface that covers him,
        get him into the folds of his bridle?
    Who could throw open the gates of his countenance?—
        his teeth cast terror all round.
    Haughty, his mighty shields,
        shut, sealed tight;
each comes right up to the other,
        no air gets between them;
        each clings to each,
           united, unparting.

41:10   His sneezes make the light shimmer;
        his eyes are like the eyelids of dawn.
    From his mouth come torches,
        fire-sparks fleeting.

His nostrils smoke
    like a pot that seethes over reeds.
His throat blazes like coals;
    his mouth emits flame.

Might resides in his neck;
    misery dances before him.
The cascades of his flesh cling,   41:15
    like cast metal on him, immovable.
Solid as rock is his heart,
    millstone-solid.
When he erupts, the gods cower,
    shrink from the waves.

Reach him with a sword and it fails,
    far-traveling spear or arrow.
Iron to him is straw;
    bronze, a rotten tree.
Arrows cannot repel him,   41:20
    fling-stones he turns to chaff;
    stubble to him, the shaft.
        He laughs at the lances' whir.

His underside is sharp shards;
    he drags a threshing sledge on the mud.
He makes the deep boil,
    the sea like soup.
Behind him gleams his wake,
    the abyss, white as an old man's head.

41:25 Nothing on dusty earth is like him,
           made not to fear.
       He gazes at lofty creatures,
           king of the haughtiest beings!

River Beast

Job answered Yahweh: 42:1

I know that You are all-powerful,
and that no plan is beyond You.

"Who dares to speak hidden words with no sense?"

I see that I spoke with no wisdom
    of things beyond me I did not know.

"Listen now and I will speak,
I will put questions, and you will inform me. . . ."

I knew You, but only by rumor;   42:5
    my eye has beheld You today.
I retract. I even take comfort
    for dust and ashes.

reborn as a phoenix?

Repentance for doubt

Job's Restoration

After Yahweh had said these things to Job, He said to Eliphaz the Temanite, "I am very angry at you and your two friends, for you have not spoken rightly about me as did my servant Job. So take seven bulls and seven rams and go to my servant Job and offer them as wholeburnt offerings for yourselves. And make sure that Job my servant prays for you; for only him will I heed not to treat you with the disgrace you deserve for not speaking rightly of me as did my servant Job." Eliphaz the Temanite and Bildad the Shuhite and Zophar the Naamatite went and did exactly what Yahweh told them to do, and Yahweh accepted Job's prayer.

42:10   Yahweh restored Job's fortunes after he prayed for his friends, doubling everything Job had.

All his brothers and sisters and all his former acquaintances came and ate bread with him in his house and mourned with him and comforted him for all the harm that Yahweh had brought upon him. Each one gave him a qesita coin and a gold ring.

Yahweh made Job more prosperous in the latter part of his life than in the former. He had fourteen thousand sheep, six thousand camels, a thousand yoke of cattle, and a thousand female donkeys, besides seven sons and three daughters. He named the first daughter Dove, and the second daughter
42:15   Cinnamon, and the third daughter Horn-of-Kohl—there were no women as beautiful as Job's daughters in all the land—and he gave them an inheritance alongside their brothers.

140

Afterward, Job lived one hundred forty years; he lived to see his sons and grandsons to the fourth generation and died in old age after a full life span.

NOTES TO THE BOOK OF JOB

The Story of Job

1:1 *Utz:* The name probably refers to a place in or near Edom, the territory to the southeast of the Dead Sea, in what is now the southern part of the Kingdom of Jordan. The exact location is less important for the literary appreciation of the book than the fact that it is non-Israelite territory. By making Job a foreigner, the author hints from the start that the story will treat a theme of universal interest, unrelated to the covenantal theology that occupies so much of the Bible.

Job: in Hebrew, *Iyyov.* The name is known from ancient Semitic inscriptions, and Ezekiel (14:14, 20) mentions it together with those of Noah and Danel (not the biblical Daniel) as that of an ancient religious hero. Although there is no certainty as to the meaning of the name, it is so similar to the common Hebrew word for enemy, *oyev,* that ears trained in Hebrew hear it as meaning "a person who is the object of enmity." This meaning is so appropriate to Job's role in the story that it may well have dictated the choice.

1:3 *men of the East:* This vague term is applied in the Bible to various peoples inhabiting territory east of the Land of Israel, including the Edomites. The East is also referred to as the location of Eden (Gen. 2:8) and the source of wisdom (I Kings 5:10). The use of the term lends the story the tone of a folktale.

1:4 *make a feast each year:* The words "each year" are strongly implied by the Hebrew. Probably it was a family ritual feast lasting seven days and celebrated each day in a different house.

1:5 *come round:* Contrary to most interpreters, I think this phrase means that Job would purify his children on the morning of the feast so that they might celebrate it in a state of ritual purity. The usual interpretation is that he would purify them after the feast in atonement for any impious words they might have let slip during their feasting.

Job would send . . . wholeburnt offerings: The performance of the ritual by the head of the family suggests that the story occurs in a patriarchal society, one more like the semilegendary world of the biblical patriarchs Abraham, Isaac, and Jacob than like the urban, hierarchical, and historically documented society of the monarchical period.

by cursing God: The word in the Hebrew text, both here and wherever the expression occurs in Job, is "bless." Expressions considered blasphemous were often replaced by antonyms, either in the original composition or by copyists. See the notes on 7:20 and 32:3.

It is not explained why, of all the sins Job might have feared his sons might have committed, he feared most that they might have cursed God. The author seems to be telling us that in addition to being punctilious in his religious observances in general, Job was particularly obsessed with speaking well of God. The author thus anticipates one of the book's main themes.

every year: The Hebrew word used here can mean "day" or "year."

1:6 lesser gods: Ancient Mediterranean literatures, both Semitic and Greek, abound in descriptions of the councils of the gods; a similar picture is found in 1 Kings 22:19–22. In the narrative of Job, in line with the monotheistic principle, Yahweh is the absolute master of the other gods, who report to Him. But by calling them lesser gods (literally, "sons of gods") rather than angels, the author strengthens the impression that the story is told by and about pagans, outside the sphere of Israelite religion.

the Accuser: The word in Hebrew is *satan.* The Hebrew word is always preceded by the definite article in Job, an indication that it had not yet become Satan of the Jewish and Christian traditions, the eternal enemy of God and man, but was still merely a title; I have therefore translated it as literally as possible. The reader must banish from his mind the more familiar image of Satan when reading the narrative of Job. The Accuser appears here as one of Yahweh's courtiers or attendants, with the particular function of keeping an eye on earth on Yahweh's behalf and reporting back on people's conduct. The model for this official may have been a functionary of the Persian secret police, known as "the eye of the king." This office was feared throughout the Persian Empire and must have been known in Judea, a province of Persia from 539 to 332 B.C. The Hebrew word *satan* is used elsewhere in the Bible to mean "enemy." Thus, the meanings of Job (popularly understood as meaning "object of enmity") and the Accuser are matched, if only by folk etymology. *Satan* is similar in sound to the word here translated as "roam," and this consonance may have suggested the wording of the Accuser's response to Yahweh's query.

1:15, 17 Sabeans: probably north Arabian nomadic marauders, rather than south Arabians from the distant kingdom of fabled wealth, home of the Queen of Sheba.

Chaldeans: This name is used in various ways in the Bible, reflecting the changes in the social condition of this people. The picture of the Chaldeans as nomadic marauders reflects their condition before the seventh century B.C., another archaizing detail in the narrative.

1:21 naked I return there: The drive for parallelism so characteristic of Hebrew and other Semitic poetry has created a logical absurdity, but one fraught with poetic beauty. We do not literally return to our mothers' wombs, but since we are born from the womb, the poet gives the same name to the place where we find our end.

2:4 Skin protecting skin!: This must be a proverbial expression. The Accuser means that Job has so far only received a skin wound, but below that skin there is other, more tender skin.

2:8 scrape . . . ashes: Scraping and sitting in ashes are mourning rituals. They may have been thought appropriate for someone stricken with certain diseases as well as with bereavement. Some of the rules laid down by Leviticus for persons suffering with skin diseases are related to the behavior of mourners (Lev. 13:45).

2:10 disgraceful: This is the normal meaning of the Hebrew word. Nearly all translations render it as "foolish." But Job judges her counsel to be not folly but wickedness. This interpretation is verified by the use of the word in connection with Job's friends in the concluding part of the frame story, 42:8.

with his lips: The text goes out of its way to stress that Job did not give voice to any anger or outrage he might have felt against God; this stress implies that his thoughts were irrelevant to his piety. In the poem, Job's bad thoughts will cross the line into speech on a massive scale.

Job's Curse

3:1 cursed his day: ironic, after we have been told so insistently that Job was always cautious in his speech.

3:3 and the night that said: Strikingly, the night itself is represented as speaking, being the only witness present at the moment of conception.

3:4 no light flood it: literally, "no light shine on it." The translation takes advantage of the fact that the rare word for "light" used here, *nehara,* also sounds like the ordinary word for "river."

3:5 deathgloom: Semitists now agree that the Hebrew word used here means simply "deep darkness" and consider the traditional interpretation that sees in it an element meaning "death" to be a folk etymology. Nevertheless, I have followed tradition in rendering this fairly common poetic word (the one that yielded the famous phrase "shadow of death" in the Authorized Version's translation of Psalm 23) "deathgloom" or "deathdark," as this more picturesque meaning is enshrined in the masoretic vocalization and is a natural association for ears accustomed to Hebrew.

3:8 men who spell the day . . . Leviathan: "Men who spell the day" are sorcerers. The Hebrew word for "day" (*yom*) is nearly the same as the name of the god of the sea in Ugaritic mythology, Yamm, which is also the Hebrew word for "ocean." The poet uses this word here with both meanings in mind so that he can represent Job as not merely cursing the day of his birth but cursing the cosmos itself. The expression "men who spell Yamm" calls to mind the ancient Canaanite myths of the victory of the god Baal over the ocean. Leviathan in our verse is the Hebrew form of the Ugaritic Lotan, the seven-headed sea monster that is another representation of the sea god defeated by Baal. Memory of such stories, variants of which were known all over the ancient world, is preserved in many passages in Job and elsewhere in the Bible. Looking back to the moment of creation, Psalms 74:13–15 describes Yahweh as the victor over the chaotic forces represented by the sea and the sea monsters, including Leviathan. And looking ahead to the end of time, Isaiah 27:1 figures Yahweh's ultimate victory over his enemies as a renewal of these primeval victories, Leviathan being explicitly named as one of the antagonists. How great a part this monster played in the imagination of the author of Job may be judged by the fact that, after naming him here at the very beginning of the poem, he brings the entire poem to a climax in 40:25–41:26 with an elaborate description of an aquatic creature called Leviathan. By invoking those who know how to stir up Leviathan, Job is actually asking for the overthrow of the order of the cosmos.

3:12 *Why did knees advance to greet me:* This phrase could refer to the knees of the midwife on whom the newly born infant was placed; or to the knees of the mother, where the infant would be held for nursing (as described in some ancient texts); or to the knees of the father, who by this ceremony would accept paternity of the child. But most vividly, perhaps the image is of the knees of the mother as they would appear to the child being born, apparently advancing to meet him as he emerged from the birth canal.

3:23 *because a god has blocked his path?:* The verb here translated as "blocked" is an ironic echo of the Hebrew word used by the Accuser in 1:10 when he admonishes Yahweh for having secured Job's loyalty by "sheltering" him from harm. The reader cannot escape the impression that Job senses that he is a victim of divine forces, though he knows nothing of the episode in heaven.

Eliphaz's First Speech

Eliphaz's point in chapters 4–5 is that Job should stop feeling sorry for himself. He has always been the one to comfort others, exhorting them with traditional wisdom, as Eliphaz is doing now. Eliphaz addresses Job gently, and does not actually accuse him of serious wrongdoing. Suffering is the lot of man because, being inherently imperfect, he is subject to punishment. But Job is basically good, so God will undoubtedly restore his fortunes; he need not fear that he will perish, for the righteous never do. Unlike many readers, I do not see any sarcasm in this, Eliphaz's first speech.

4:3 *You were always the one to instruct the many:* To comfort mourners with pious exhortations was a duty of leadership, as we shall see in 29:25.

4:10 *The lion roars!:* Eliphaz's image of the ignominious decline of the blustering wicked man, like so much of the book's imagery, is taken from the world of nature. The forests that once existed in the Land of Israel and the lions with which they abounded figure prominently both in biblical poetry and prose. The author of Job was able to deploy five different words for lion in this passage, while the English translator has to make do with one.

The image of the lions roaring in pride and later suffering in famine anticipates the image of the fool and his brief prosperity to be described by the angel-apparition in the dream sequence that follows.

4:12 *Now, word has reached me in stealth:* Eliphaz's night vision is one of the most evocative passages in the book. Another night vision will be described much less elaborately by Elihu in 33:15. Unlike most interpreters, I think that Eliphaz's mysterious apparition continues speaking until 5:7 instead of ending at the close of chapter 4.

5:2–5 *Remember: Only fools are killed by anger . . . and thirsty men gulp his wealth:* As is evident from the translation, I do not think that these verses refer to the punishment of sinners, which is the usual explanation. I understand the apparition's message to be that human fortunes fluctuate because man is inherently imperfect. If we agonize over this reality, we are wasting our breath, and protests like Job's curse in chapter 3 are ineffectual.

5:5 *his wealth:* an emendation for "their wealth."

5:7 *as sparks dart to the sky:* The Hebrew phrase translated as "sparks" means, literally, "the sons of Reshef." Reshef is the name of a well-known Canaanite deity that appears reduced to the status of a common noun several times in the Bible. In some of these passages, the context suggests that it was used to mean "pestilence"; in others, "flame"; and once, "arrows." If the correct meaning here is "flame," "the sons of flame" would seem to be sparks.

5:8 *No, I look to El:* Eliphaz now draws the moral from his vision. God is all-powerful and ultimately just, so Job should do as Eliphaz does and put his trust in Him. Eliphaz's ecstatic hymn beginning here is echoed by Job himself in chapter 9, where it is invested with quite different emotional content.

5:19 *In six-times-trouble . . . in seven:* Proverbial expressions and poetry are often built on arbitrarily chosen pairs of ascending numbers in biblical Hebrew and other Canaanite languages. Job himself uses this device effectively in his response to Yahweh's first speech (40:5): "One time I spoke;/I will not speak again;/Two times I spoke,/and I will not go on."

5:24 *You will be sure of peace in your household:* The two words for "household" in the Hebrew text (the second of which is here represented by the pronoun "it") are metonymies for "wife." Whenever he "visits" her, Job will find her willing and himself potent, so that he will unfailingly impregnate her. This interpretation links the verse quite naturally to the promise of fertility and of undiminished vigor in the following verses; it also makes the image of the sprouting grass more pointed.

5:26 *Still robust . . . :* The promise for the righteous is that they will die not in pain and decrepitude but in full vigor, like Moses in the last verses of Deuteronomy.

Job's Reply to Eliphaz's First Speech

Eliphaz's reassuring prognostication at the end of chapter 5 can only have irritated the suffering Job, who must also have been annoyed by Eliphaz's roundabout way of putting his criticism of Job into the mouth of an apparition. Now Job attacks Eliphaz for being all words and no deeds.

Job's reply to Eliphaz's first speech is in two parts: a tirade against Eliphaz and the other friends mixed with expressions of personal bitterness, and an emotional statement about the nature of human life and suffering. Job's reply in these chapters is still dominated by the theme of chapter 3, that death would be preferable to this kind of life.

6:5–6 *Is that a wild ass . . . mallows?:* These sentences are usually taken as proverbial expressions such as: Does the ass bray over his grass? Does the ox bellow over his feed? Can unsalted food be eaten? and so on. I follow Marvin H. Pope's commentary in understanding them to be sarcastic descriptions of the speeches of Job's antagonists.

6:9–10 *if that god . . . crush me . . . comfort me:* I.e., if God would kill me, that would be a comfort.

6:10 *for never have I suppressed the Holy One's commands:* God owes Job at least this much.

6:13–14 *Is there no help within myself . . . Shaddai?:* These two lines are famously obscure in the Hebrew; but although Job is not being altogether coherent, a thread of reason can be discerned in his remarks here. Having been driven to the limit of endurance, knowing that he can expect no help from God or true comfort from his friends, he tries to assure himself that as long as his reason holds he can find equilibrium or perhaps at least solve his problem through suicide. But all translations here are conjectural; my contribution is to run the lines together into a single syntactic unit.

6:16 *Gloomy on an icy day . . . :* The image of the wadi recurs frequently in the book, as it does throughout the Bible. A wadi is a desert watercourse that is dry much of the year but that can suddenly be filled with a torrential flow of water. The brief passage of water often leaves behind a growth of refreshing flowers and grasses; hence, the wadi may serve as an image of comfort and rest. But travelers using a wadi as a road are sometimes overtaken by such torrents and drowned; hence, the wadi may serve as an image of treachery. The appearance of a wadi from afar heartens the desert traveler, who heads for it in hope of finding a little water at the bottom of its channel. In this, he is often disappointed; hence, the wadi may serve as an image of unreliability. That, in my opin-ion, is the image intended by Job in this passage.

6:19 Tema . . . Sabean trains: Tema and Sabea are two oases in northwest Arabia.

6:20 find frustration: like the translator, who is forced to aban-don hope of translating the double entendre; for the verb used here means "to dig" as well as "to be frustrated."

6:21 That is how you are to me: adopting the nearly universally accepted emendation of "to him" to "to me."

6:25 How eloquent are honest words: Job contrasts his words of honest complaint with Eliphaz's routine eloquence.

6:26 Do you think you can teach me with words?: alluding to Eliphaz's repeated use of the word "words" at the beginning of his opening speech. Nearly at the end of his introduction, Job is warming up to the main part of his speech, which comes in chap-ter 7.

6:29 Come back . . . Come back!: This call almost sounds like a buried stage direction, as if the friends were so offended by Job's attack on them in the preceding verses that they got up to leave. Such suggestions of action are scattered throughout the book—e.g., 17:10 and 18:2.

7:1 Man's life on earth . . . : Eliphaz's fatuous attempt at conso-lation at the end of chapter 5 has spurred Job to reflect a bit more systematically, and now, after his opening tirade, he makes his first general statement about the nature of human life and suffering. But this statement, rooted as it is in his own experience, is hardly more dispassionate than his tirade against Eliphaz. It is punctuat-ed by outbursts directed against God Himself.

Eliphaz had implied that Job was suffering because he had sinned. Job now observes that he is not the only sufferer, for man in general was born to a short and hard life. He does not claim to be completely innocent; he admits he is human and subject to error. His question is, why should God care so much? It would be fairer if God let man alone, for there is no sin that puny man could possibly commit that could threaten or harm God in any way. Job does not distinguish here between his lot and the lot of mankind at large; he considers his own suffering to be merely an extreme case. Job will return to this theme, giving it a more universalized treatment, in chapter 14.

The speech is divided into two parts by the expression "and I'll be gone," near the midpoint and at the end.

7:15 *death is better than this misery:* The translation is based on a slight emendation of the Hebrew text, which, as it stands, yields "better than my bones."

7:20 *a burden to myself?:* An ancient Jewish tradition maintains that this passage originally read "a burden to You" but was altered by ancient scribes to avoid seeming to attribute weakness to God. But the text actually makes better sense in its present form. For another case of euphemistic emendations by scribes, see the comment on 1:5.

Bildad's First Speech

Bildad centers the discussion on merit, but directly accuses only Job's sons of sinning. He emphasizes the frailty of the wicked man's successes and assures Job of restoration if he will only acknowledge his guilt. Bildad's thoughts in this chapter are mostly organized around the death of Job's sons and his loss thereby of hope to be remembered in his own place. This problem is implicitly raised again at the speech's end, in the image of the ruinous vine, and it cannot be far from Bildad's mind when he cites the wisdom of earlier generations.

8:8 *Just ask the older generation:* Bildad cites as his authority the wisdom of the ancients, using a formula found elsewhere in the Bible. "The wisdom of the ancients" is the body of maxims, poems, and parables for proper conduct, for survival, and for understanding the order of the universe. Bits of such wisdom were compiled in books, like the biblical book of Proverbs; some of these books were designed for the education of government officials or princes. By tracing his ideas back to tradition, Bildad lends his speech a somewhat objective character, in contrast to Eliphaz in chapters 4–5, who spoke largely in his own voice and drew on personal experience.

8:10 *from memory:* literally, "from their hearts." The translation reflects Bildad's point that the elders' wisdom derives not merely from momentary feelings but from observations passed down through many generations and originating in dim antiquity.

8:12 *even before the grass:* The tall, stately papyrus plant withers at the end of summer, when the lowly grass is still green.

8:16 *Juicy green before the sun:* The image of the vine beginning here represents the prosperity of the wicked; it is not a grapevine but a creeper growing over an abandoned site, not a healthy growth but a sign of decay.

8:19 *Such is his happy lot:* Bildad turns to Job as he says these words, then turns back to complete his parable.

8:21 *He will yet:* This translation necessitates emending a single vowel.

Job's Reply to Bildad's First Speech

Job's great speech in chapters 9–10 introduces one of the book's major themes: his fantasy of facing God and demanding justice in a court of law. From the beginning, Job knows just how absurd it is to entertain such a fantasy, yet he returns to it again and again, and it is the last theme in his mouth when the discussion finally ends, in chapter 31.

Job begins this magnificent speech by acknowledging God's power over nature. God overwhelmed the ocean monster; how, then, can a mere mortal hope to best Him in argument? Yet Job insists on his innocence. He can only conclude that when evil flourishes, it is because God tolerates it. Contrary to Bildad's bland assurances, God does pervert justice! Passages of rage at God's injustice alternate with passages of self-pity.

But God is not only the all-powerful victor over nature's forces; He also is the author of Job's life. As such, He should have a stake in Job's life, and an interest in protecting him. Why would He grant him the gift of life and then torment him? It would have been better to have died in the womb. Job concludes by wishing that since God has created him mortal, He should at least let him alone to spend his few days in peace.

9:2 *that this is so:* Job here agrees with Bildad that those God deems wicked suffer and those God deems righteous prosper. What angers him is that God does not determine justly who is wicked and who is righteous, and there is no way to persuade or compel Him to do so.

9:3 *If someone chose to challenge Him, He . . . :* If man chose to accuse God, God would refuse to answer one in a thousand of the accusations; but the Hebrew could also mean that if God chose to quarrel with man, man would be unable to answer.

9:4 *Shrewd or powerful:* These two adjectives are usually taken to refer to God, as if saying, "He is shrewd and powerful."

9:5-10 *He moves the mountains . . . :* Job's little hymn on God's might beginning here echoes that of Eliphaz in chapter 5, and even quotes it verbatim in the verse "He makes things great beyond man's grasp,/and wonders beyond any numbering." But whereas Eliphaz's hymn was adoring, Job's expresses man's anxiety at contemplating God's powers of destruction.

9:5-11 *and they are unaware . . . and I am unaware:* God's brutal treatment of unthinking nature has no more moral content than His treatment of man. Likewise, man is ordinarily no more conscious of God's control over his life than are the dumb mountains of His control over the forces of nature.

9:8 *and treads Yamm's back:* another reference to the primeval sea monster vanquished by Baal; see the notes to chapter 3.

9:9 *the South Wind's chambers:* The assumption here, as in 37:9, seems to be that each wind is stored, until use, in a chamber of its own.

9:13 *Rahab's cohorts:* Rahab is another name for the sea monster vanquished by God in primeval times. The name is known only from mythological remnants in the Bible. The "cohorts" recall the helpers of Tiamat, who was vanquished by Marduk in the parallel Babylonian myth.

9:19 *Who can summon Him?:* The Hebrew text reads "who can summon *me*?"; this translation is made possible by a very slight emendation.

9:21 *I am good . . . life:* These three short sentences present no grammatical or lexical difficulties, but their connection is obscure. Perhaps they represent Job as briefly thrown into verbal confusion by the vehemence of his feelings and the daring of the thoughts that are forcing themselves on him.

9:26 *skiffs of reed:* The reed from which boats were made, especially in Egypt, was papyrus. Such boats were proverbial for speed, as may be seen from the reference to them in Isaiah 18:2.

9:27 *breathe a while:* The translation attempts to balance the traditional explanation of the obscure verb as meaning "take strength" and the consensus of modern and some medieval scholars that the word has something to do with joy or pleasure.

9:30 *liquid snow:* Modern commentators correctly, if literal-mindedly, point out that liquid snow is not a detergent like lye, referred to in the parallel clause; accordingly, they define the Hebrew word so translated as "soapwort," a root from which soap was made, and the name of which in later Hebrew texts happens to resemble the Hebrew word for "snow." I am sticking to the traditional explanation, as being more poetic and recalling a famous reference to snow in Isaiah 1:18.

9:35 *His presence:* based on a minuscule emendation of the suffix denoting the pronoun.

10:8–9 *kneaded:* The usual meaning of this verb is "made"; but it is very similar to a verb meaning "to squeeze" and to a later Hebrew noun meaning "dough." In view of the imagery of cooking, baking, and eating in the following verses, I think the verb here may be translated as "knead."

10:13 *Yet all these things . . . :* Perhaps Job means that God has grudgingly kept track of His benefactions to man mentioned in the preceding verses; thus, when man commits some little wrong, God's rage seems to be beyond all reasonable measure. Alternatively, Job might be referring to all the little things he may have done wrong, as he goes on to explain in the following verses.

10:15 *drenched:* based on the emendation of one consonant.

10:16 *pleased with Yourself:* God hunts him like a lion, then withdraws to enjoy the sight of Job's terror. The root means "something marvelous, extraordinary," and the verbal form in which it appears here is often reflexive in meaning. I therefore think it can bear the meaning "to find oneself wonderful," hence this translation. This semantic development has a parallel in Arabic.

10:17 *enmity:* The word thus rendered normally means "witnesses," but it is hard to see how that would fit the context. The rendering "hostility" suggested by a few modern scholars is justified by reference to a similar-sounding Arabic root.

    so my travail is constantly renewed: The sentence in Hebrew means "replacement and hardship with me." My translation results from taking the two nouns as a hendiadys, a figure of speech in which two words linked by a conjunction yield a single complex meaning, like "nice and warm," meaning, "nicely warm." The usage of the two nouns, when they recur together in 14:14 (though not in a hendiadys), tends to confirm this interpretation.

10:20 *catch my breath:* See the note on "breathe a while" at 9:27.

10:22 *where You blaze forth . . . :* This clause is generally understood to mean that Sheol, the region described in these lines, is a place so disordered and chaotic that in it darkness and light are mixed. But since the verb could equally well be in the second-person singular, I take it to mean that it is God who shines forth in Sheol; this interpretation yields the paradoxical and terrifying image in the translation.

Zophar's First Speech

Speaking last of the three friends in this first round of speeches, Zophar takes up Job's demand for a personal confrontation with God. If God were to appear, says Zophar, it would not be in a litigation; it would be a revelation that would reveal to Job how limited is human understanding, how unable to grasp the subtlety of God's judgment. After touching lightly on this important theme, which will be further developed later in the book, Zophar goes back to urging Job to reject his former ways, assuring him of a prosperous future if he does so.

11:3 *restrains:* rather than "rebukes," as in most interpretations. This form of the verb occurs in two other biblical passages (Judg. 18:7 and Ruth 2:15).

11:10 *Should He pass by, confine, or confiscate:* This obscure verse has inspired various interpretations. The verb translated as "confine" could also mean "hand over"; the verb translated as "confiscate" could also mean "assemble."

11:11 *could He see wrong and look the other way?:* This question may be in answer to Job's complaint that God pays undue attention to his minor failings, as in 7:18ff.

Job's Reply to Zophar's First Speech

Job's reply to Zophar in chapters 12–14 concludes the first round of the discussion between Job and his three friends. His address falls into several parts. In 12:1 to 13:5, Job subjects the friends to his lengthiest and most sarcastic attack so far, deriding, in light of his own hard experience, their claim to the wisdom of the ancients. From 13:6 to 13:16, he invites the friends to listen to his address to God. From 13:17 to the end of chapter 14, he indulges his fantasy of a courtroom confrontation with God, addressing God directly as if accusing Him. But in the course of his address, the tone suddenly shifts from accusation to lamentation, for much of chapter 14 consists of sorrowful reflections on the nature of human life and suffering. That chapter, among the most beautiful in the book, has the feel of an independent poem; in context, it may be regarded as Job's chief piece of evidence in support of his accusation against God.

12:4 *"He calls to God and He answers him!":* possibly an allusion to the taunt at 5:1; cf. the famous taunt in Psalms 22:9, "He trusted on the Lord that He would deliver him: let Him deliver him, seeing He delighted in him" (quoted from the AV).

12:6 *Highway robbers' . . . :* Perhaps the meaning is that they are confident of their ill-gotten prosperity. I cannot accept the notion of many interpreters that the passage refers to idolaters and is to be translated as "for those who bring their God in their hand."

12:7 *But just ask . . . :* Job attacks the friends' claim to ancient wisdom, as enunciated by Bildad in chapter 8, by parodying that very style. Even the beasts of the field know that God wields tyrannical power over everything. The wisdom of the elders is insignificant compared with that of God; in fact, God often turns elders, with their pretensions to wisdom, into raving fools. In another context, this paean to God's wisdom might have been a hymn of praise. Here, it expresses rage at God's tyranny and scorn for the three friends.

12:9 *that Yahweh's hand has done all this:* "This" must refer to all that has befallen Job. People like Job's friends may laugh at him and explain his misfortunes in any way they like, but any animal knows that God is completely arbitrary, that He is the source of chaos as well as of order.

The appearance of the name of Yahweh, the deity of the ancient Hebrews, is a striking exception to the author's regular practice, for this is the only occurrence of the name in the speeches of Job and his friends. (The name does occur in the narrative portions of the book, and Yahweh appears in person in chapters 38–41.) Some ancient Bible manuscripts have here, instead of Yahweh, the word *eloah,* the word most commonly used in Job for god or God. Since the same clause appears in Isaiah 41:20 with the name Yahweh (cf. also Ps. 109:27), some explain its occurrence in this passage by conjecturing that the word *eloah* originally appeared here but was altered to correspond to the wording in Isaiah; others conjecture that this passage is quoted from Isaiah verbatim. But the word used for God here does not affect the argument of the passage, for Job and his friends often use *eloah* to refer to the one master of the universe rather than one god among many.

12:11–12 *"The ear . . . perspicacious":* These verses are maxims meaning "Experience is what counts." Job quotes them in order to shoot them down in the following verses, which contrast God's vast wisdom with man's insignificant experience.

12:13 He *has wisdom and power*: Here begins an extraordinary parody of hymnic style. God is the author not only of wonders but of chaos and breakdown.

12:17–19 *He makes counselors go mad . . . priests go mad*: The meaning of the word here translated as "go mad" is, literally, "stripped." Commentators differ as to what the counselors and priests are stripped of. I follow the traditional opinion that it is their reason.

12:18 *unties the bonds of kings*: I have left it somewhat ambiguous, as in the Hebrew; the meaning seems to be that He undoes the authority of kings, since the noun used here can mean both "chastisement" and "bond."

though He Himself had bound the sash about their waists: The sash is the sash of the warrior, bound tightly as he goes into battle, therefore symbolizing the ruler, whose authority derives from his martial prowess.

12:19 *eternal truths*: All commentators interpret the noun used here as referring to another group of people, parallel to the authority figures of the preceding verses; but there is no agreement as to what group is meant. The word means "something unfailing"; since the verb used here as the predicate is ordinarily applied to speech rather than to persons, it seems to me that Job is using it to refer to maxims like the ones he himself cited a few verses earlier as examples of the unreliability of human wisdom. If God undermines the natural and political order at will, why not the epistemological order as well? The question is particularly pointed here because the friends, as representatives of the wisdom tradition, have nothing to offer but the "eternal" wisdom of maxims.

12:23 *spreads traps for other nations, but guides them safely*: The verb in the first clause means, literally, "He spreads"; but the verse does not say what He spreads. Many commentators take it to mean that God expands their territory, but this would not contrast with the second clause. I assume "traps" to be the implied direct object; thus, the second part of the verse is in chiastic parallelism with the first (i.e., the semantically equivalent words are in *abba* order: God elevates and destroys; traps and guides safely).

13:1–5 Look . . . that would be wisdom!: Job reverts from indirect attacks on his friends to the directness with which he had attacked them at the beginning of his address, and he repeats some of his earlier language. He concludes the first part of his address by expressing the wish that they would just be quiet.

13:6 Listen to my accusation: Here begins the second part of Job's speech, as Job invites the friends to attend his day in court with God; the language becomes much more ceremonious than that of the first part of Job's speech, and it employs many terms associated with judicial procedures used elsewhere in the Bible. Among these are the summonses to attention that punctuate this passage and serve as cues to its segmentation. They recall the solemn opening of Moses' farewell poem, Deuteronomy 32:1: "Listen, O heavens, and I will speak! Let the earth hear the words of my mouth"; and the beginning of Isaiah's rebuke (Isa. 1:2): "Listen, O heavens! Give ear, O earth!" The word meaning "complaint" in this verse is a typical courtroom term; the same Hebrew word underlies the phrase "argue on El's behalf" a few lines further on.

13:7–8 Will you speak falsehood for the sake of El . . . show partiality . . . argue on El's behalf?: I.e., by defending God, you are lying on His behalf, behavior that God would not tolerate in a human court. "Show partiality" is an idiomatic rendering of the Hebrew expression "to lift up faces," behavior condemned in Proverbs 18:5 and described as alien to God's ways in Deuteronomy 10:17. "Argue on El's behalf" strikingly recalls the dramatic confrontation in Judges 6:31.

13:11 if He were to loom: literally, "at his arising." The noun is used to mean the emergence into view of something imposing or terrifying, like Leviathan in 41:17; cf. 31:23.

13:14 Why am I carrying . . . hands?: The meaning is, "Why am I being so cautious, so self-protective?"

13:15 Let Him kill me!—I will never flinch: The familiar translation in the Authorized Version, "Though He slay me, yet will I trust in Him," is based on a variant of the Hebrew text. Its moving expression of trust in God's beneficence is completely at variance with Job's attitude in this chapter and in the rest of the poem.

His conduct: I have taken the liberty of making a small emendation so that this word refers to God's conduct rather than to Job's, as stated in the Hebrew text. This emendation is necessary because the verb in the sentence cannot mean "to defend," as it is normally rendered here; it means "to accuse," "to reproach," as it does in its many other occurrences in Job. The whole context shows that what Job intends to do is to attack God for His ways. That is why Job's speech is so dangerous, and why he half expects God to retaliate.

13:16 *for flatterers can never come before Him:* Dripping with sarcasm, Job defies God to retaliate against him for speaking, thereby breaking with His own standards of strict justice in the courtroom. Cf. Psalms 101:7.

13:17 *all who hear me:* I have added these words in order to clarify that the addressee in this verse is not God, as the verb inflections have turned from singular to plural.

13:21 *Take Your palm away from me . . . fear of You:* Cf. 9:34.

13:26 *bitter deed:* This Hebrew word, meaning, literally, "bitter things," sounds similar to a word that means "rebellion." It may be that a conflation of the two words has yielded the meaning it bears here.

13:27 *mark the roots of my feet:* The Hebrew text is quite obscure; the verb probably means "to make a mark," "to engrave." (In modern Hebrew, the verb means "to track someone," but this usage derives from the interpretation of this very verse and so is not helpful to us.) No satisfactory interpretation has been proposed.

13:28 has been displaced; it belongs after 14:2.

14:1 *Man born of woman:* Job's reflections that begin here, a lamentation on man's condition, raise the discussion to a whole new level. Job's personal sufferings are no longer the issue; through them, he reaches an acute understanding of the insubstantiality of human life and gives it poignant expression. We saw Job embarking on this train of thought in his response to Eliphaz's first speech (chap. 7), but then the acuteness of his own suffering prevented him from developing the idea. In his reply to Bildad (chaps. 9–10), the theme of man's tragedy was stronger, but it was dominated by Job's resentment of God's perversion of justice and intrusion on man's life. Here, the theme of the human tragedy predominates, interrupted occasionally by references to Job's personal situation.

The contentiousness that has prevailed until this point suddenly disappears, along with the courtroom imagery, and the tone turns elegiac. Some scholars consider this chapter to be an independent poem that was inserted into Job's speech.

This phrase, "man born of woman," means simply, "mortal man." It was not intended to refer to the doctrine of original sin, which was read back into the Old Testament by early Christian religious thinkers, nor need it have anything to do with the rules of ritual impurity (Lev. 12), as contended by some academic readers.

14:3 *Do You call a man like me to judgment against You?:* In chapter 13, Job had demanded a court trial; this inconsistency also suggests that the poem in chapter 14 is taken from a separate source.

14:4 *Who can purify a thing impure?:* This sounds like a proverbial expression, similar to our "You cannot make a sow's ear into a silk purse." Job uses it to mean that God wants to hold him to the standard of perfection, when he is but an imperfect mortal. There are several ironies in the use of this proverb. The impure often *can* be made pure, through prescribed ritual actions, but nothing can make man immortal or perfect. Furthermore, God could have made man perfect, if He had chosen to do so. This verse is thus an irritable intrusion on the prevailing elegiac tone.

14:5 *and You have set him bounds he cannot cross:* Similar expressions are used several times in the Bible; for example, the seashore is described as a limit to the ocean (Ps. 104:9), and the firmament as a limit to the upper waters (Ps. 148:6).

14:6 *let him be!:* literally, "Stop!"—a minuscule emendation of the text, which reads, "Let him stop." The same imperative occurs in 7:16 and 10:20.

14:13 *If You would only hide me . . . :* In these verses, Job "gropes toward the idea of an afterlife" (Pope's formulation). Job and his friends generally take for granted the standard Old Testament view that there is no real survival after death, only a realm in which the shades of the dead carry on a vague existence without any clear sensations. But in the urgency of his need for justice, Job here briefly hits on the germ of a solution (suggested by his thoughts about the tree in the preceding passage): a temporary period in Sheol followed by resurrection. That would give man at least as much hope as a dead tree stump. But he quickly dismisses this fantasy. Later religious thinkers would develop the idea of resurrection into a pillar of both Judaism and Christianity.

14:16 *see nothing but my sins:* The Hebrew text has "You do not observe my sins"; like some other readers, I have altered the meaning to fit the context.

14:17 *sealed up in a bundle:* In His enmity toward Job, God has taken personal pains to preserve his sins like precious documents or money.

14:19 *torrents:* The Hebrew text reads "aftergrowth," which makes no sense. The solution, accepted even by medieval commentators, involves the transposition of two letters.

14:22 *he mourns himself alone:* The word "alone" has two functions. The dead man in Sheol has no knowledge of what transpires among the living, so he has nothing to do but mourn himself; and the living have no knowledge of him, so he is the only one to mourn.

Eliphaz's Second Speech

Eliphaz begins his second speech by mocking Job and deprecating his supposed wisdom, assuring him that his own message is based on authentic ancient wisdom. He repeats the thought so dramatically delivered in his first speech (chap. 4) that no man can be completely innocent, since God does not even trust His own angels. The body of his speech is an extended description of the fate of the wicked man, stressing the anxiety that is his lot.

15:2 *hot air from the East:* The East is the source of the sirocco, the parching desert wind that symbolizes barrenness. But the East is also the traditional source of wisdom (cf. Job 1:3 and the note thereto). These conflicting connotations produce sarcasm.

15:8 overhear the gods in council: Councils of the gods are frequently described in the Middle Eastern myths preserved in Egyptian, Ugaritic, Akkadian, and Greek. In the Bible, the image of a convivial gathering of immortals has mostly been attenuated into scenes of a divine court, where Yahweh is attended by His courtiers, who are portrayed as His servants, as in I Kings 22:19–22 and in the first two chapters of Job; a vestige of the polytheistic version remains in those passages of the creation story in which God speaks in the first-person plural. Cf. Genesis 1:26; 11:7.

15:11 pious consolations: literally, "the consolations of El," or, simply, "divine consolations." Eliphaz is, of course, referring to his own efforts and those of Bildad and Zophar to comfort and counsel Job. Words of comfort may be considered divine words both in the sense that to console a mourner is a pious duty, as well as in the sense that such consolation has religious teaching as its content; see the head note to chapter 4.

15:12 heart . . . eyes: These organs are traditionally considered seductive betrayers that lead man to sin; see Numbers 15:39.

15:14–16 How can mortal man be guiltless . . . guzzles sin like water?: Eliphaz has said this already in his first speech (4:17). Too tactful to state outright that Job must have sinned, he pointed out that all creatures, even the angels, are sinful. When, in his last speech, Job spoke pathetically of man's mortality (14:1), his words echoed those of Eliphaz. Now Eliphaz tries to shake Job out of his self-pity and lead him to repentance by stressing not man's mortality but his propensity to sin.

15:18 things that wise men used to tell: As in his first speech, Eliphaz is careful to claim higher authority for his wisdom. This time, he follows Zophar's lead in citing tradition as the authority. He traces his doctrine back to primeval times, when the world was simple, when people kept to their own kind, when wisdom was undiluted.

15:20 All the days of the wicked man: In this speech, Eliphaz describes the punishment of the wicked man as something internal. The wicked man is punished, above all, with anxiety: He is frightened of the sounds in his own ears and feels himself attacked in peacetime; he is unsure of his security, anticipates the sword, doubts his sustenance, and is anxious about war. In the same way, Eliphaz targets Job's conscience, declaring that Job's own lips proclaim his guilt.

15:24 straits and hardship: He is as terrified by the thought of deprivation as of a military attack; a real man would arm himself against want by summoning his powers of endurance.

15:24 assault: There is no consensus among scholars as to the exact meaning of the Hebrew word thus translated.

15:29 his fullness: another of the book's obscurities.

15:33 he drops his still-unripe fruit, like a vine: probably means that the wicked man loses his children while they are still young, with the additional connotation that they were sour fruit to begin with. The image is slightly problematic, since unripe grapes cling more tightly to the vine than do ripe ones. But in this parable, the vine itself is unhealthy.

like an olive tree: The normal olive tree does shed its blossoms in spring in an impressive display, but very few of the blossoms produce fruit. The parable must mean that the wicked are not blessed with profuse progeny.

15:35 men conceiving . . . deceit: a striking variation on the well-worn idea that the wicked are punished with barrenness; the poet turns the wicked men into women and the fruit of their wombs into an abstraction.

Job's Reply to Eliphaz's Second Speech

Job begins this speech with the usual expressions of resentment against the friends and their brand of consolation, but he makes an unexpected shift, addressing his complaint to God. Soon he is attacking both God and the friends, portraying all of them as responsible for his suffering. The complaint about the three friends broadens into a general complaint about Job's fall from his social position, even his exclusion from commercial life. About midway through the speech (16:22), Job reverts to the theme of the brevity of life, which is never far from his mind. But in his exasperation, he lapses into near incoherence, as ideas and images tumble out of him in disorder. These two chapters are dense with obscurities.

16:2 *all three:* literally, "all of you."

16:4–5 *If you were in my place . . . spare my lips no mumbling motion:* The Hebrew lacks the expected negative particle before "motion." By emphasizing the physical organs of speech, Job alludes to the superficiality of his friends' attempts to console him. Job means to say that if the friends were the sufferers and he the comforter, he would do a better job; but in saying so, he cannot resist a bit of sarcasm.

16:7–8 *You have . . . my company, crumpled me:* The verbs in this sentence are singular, so it must be addressed to God. "Company" may refer to Job's family or to his intimates. "Crumpled" has something to do with destruction, but its connotations are unknown; in its only other occurrence in the Bible, Job 22:16, I translated it simply as "destroyed." "Crumpled" here was suggested by the sound of the Hebrew word.

16:8 *my witness:* The theme of the witness becomes important at the end of the chapter, but its meaning here is unclear. Perhaps Job is speaking, in rage and sarcasm, from the friends' point of view: To them, his emaciation and other symptoms are a witness *against* him, testifying that he must have sinned.

16:9 *He rends:* In the passage beginning here, Job describes his sufferings as an attack on himself by warriors and wild beasts.

16:12–17 *I was at peace . . . and though my prayer is pure:* This passage is replete with rhythmic and acoustic effects that are only partly amenable to imitation in another language.

16:15 *dug my horns into the dirt:* The image is of an animal that has collapsed with its horns—its weapon and the insignia of its pride—dug into the ground.

16:18 *O Earth! Do not conceal my blood . . . place to rest!:* This outburst is Job's plea that the outrage done him never be forgotten and forgiven. The effacement by time of the guilt caused by murder is figuratively represented by the absorption into the earth of spilled blood. When God wants to tell Cain that his brother Abel's blood is awaiting vengeance, He says (Gen. 4:10): "The voice of your brother's blood is crying out to me from the ground." For a further elaboration of the image, see Ezekiel 24:7–8. This image was translated into ritual, for covering the blood with dirt was the procedure for rendering the meat of hunted animals fit for eating (Lev. 17:13). The second image, the plea that Job's voice forever soar restlessly throughout the world, reminding mankind of his unavenged cause, is an equivalent parallel.

16:20 *Such advocates!:* This word can also be understood as meaning "scorners"; hence, AV's "My friends scorn me."

17:3 *"Take my security!"—"There's my pledge!"—"Who will do business with me?":* Job began this speech by complaining about his faithless friends, and he is now extending this complaint to one about his general isolation from society. He is so ostracized that he cannot even conduct normal commercial transactions; as he lies in bed, his own futile supplications to other merchants and the memory of their silent refusal to deal with him ring in his ears.

17:4 *You will not let them rise:* This is a literal translation of the Hebrew, but its significance is unknown.

17:5 *"If one tells . . . languish":* probably a proverbial expression, which Job cites and applies to himself, reproaching himself for speaking frankly to his three friends. "Will languish" might be a scribal error for "will darken," a difference of a single letter; two verses later, Job says that his own eyes have darkened.

17:6 *I have turned . . . faces:* "Spittle" is only a guess, an onomatopoeic interpretation of the Hebrew word (*tofet*). Job imagines that when people see him, they think of the proverbial expression just cited, and they spit, either out of contempt for him or to ward off the harm they see him suffering.

17:8–9 *Men of goodwill . . . the righteous man:* i.e., Job himself, who holds to his way, despite his suffering at the hands of both God and men.

17:10, 12 *all three . . . the face of darkness:* Job again calls his friends to return when they seem to be on the point of walking out on his discourse, as in 6:28–29. I have substituted "all three" for the plural pronoun, as in verse 2. I have also reversed the order of verses 11 and 12 for clarity's sake.

17:12 *pretend that light is closer than:* This translation is made possible by emending "in the face of" to "than," a change of a single letter. The friends act as if Job's troubles were practically over, for all he has to do is acknowledge his guilt and all will be well.

Bildad's Second Speech

Bildad begins by exhorting his two colleagues to try again. The body of his speech resumes the theme of Eliphaz's last discourse with a description of the fate in store for the wicked.

18:2 *you two:* The Hebrew simply has "you" (plural); since Bildad clearly does not mean to include Job, he must be addressing Eliphaz and Zophar.

keep speech at an end: This phrase echoes the opening lines of Job's last speech (16:3). It creates the impression that, after Job's preceding, nearly incoherent speech, with its mixed expressions of anguish and attacks on the three friends, there followed an embarrassed silence.

18:4 *You . . . :* This apostrophe marks Bildad's turning toward Job. His point is that Job should not think for a moment that his sufferings mean that the world has been abandoned and is without justice.

or the cliff dislodged from its place: an echo of Job's own words in 14:18.

18:8 *for he has been sent off with nets:* Here begins a little poem made up of variations on the image of trapping.

18:9 *Traps hold him fast:* Unfortunately, there is no certainty, only consensus based on context, as to the meaning of the word here translated as "traps."

18:12 *His strength . . . at his side:* With deep regret, I am rejecting a traditional interpretation of this verse, according to which the noun rendered as "strength" is equivalent to "son," and the noun rendered as "side" is equivalent to "wife." The former identification was suggested to the ancient commentators by the usage of the word in Deuteronomy 21:17; the latter, by the role of the rib in the story of the fashioning of Eve from Adam's side. As lovely as this interpretation is, and though it fits the context admirably, it is simply too midrashic in style to fit my criteria for translation.

18:13 *sticks:* i.e., the bones, all that is left of the sinner's emaciated body after the starvation of the preceding verse.

the Firstborn of Death: While we have no exact information about the identity of this figure or of that of the King of Terror in the next verse, it seems probable that they are vestiges of ancient myths. The Canaanite god of the underworld, corresponding to Nergal in Akkadian myth and Pluto in Greek myth, was named Mot, i.e., "death"; he is referred to elsewhere in the Bible (Ps. 49:15; Jer. 9:20). Pope conjectures that "the King of Terror" is an epithet of Mot. It is not hard to imagine that a particular cause of death might have been referred to as a son of Mot; similar idioms are quite common in Arabic.

18:15 *Now his tent dwells:* The pronoun in the Hebrew is feminine, which may be what led ancient commentators to discover a wife in verse 12. I have changed it to masculine and dropped an intrusive preposition, since there is no feminine subject in the vicinity.

18:20 *Latter-day men:* Ruins often stimulated people of the ancient Middle East to brood on the brevity of life and the evanescence of worldly glory. In the Bible, the image of people of later ages taking a lesson from Israel's ruins figures in prophetic admonitions (cf. Deut. 29:21–27). In service of the general theme of mortality, the theme remained active in Arabic poetry through the Middle Ages and rejoined Hebrew literature in a striking poem by Samuel the Nagid (see my book *Wine, Women, and Death: Medieval Hebrew Poems on the Good Life* [Philadelphia: Jewish Publication Society, 1986], pp. 154–57).

Job's Reply to Bildad's Second Speech

This speech of Job's, though passionate, is more controlled than his last one. After the opening address to the friends, it falls into two parts. The first takes up his complaint about his condition; it contains a striking depiction of the way in which his domestic life has been affected by the loss of dignity consequent on his sufferings. In the second part, he takes up the theme with which Bildad had concluded: the thought of how Job's story will be regarded in times to come. Job has given up, for the time being, on the idea of a confrontation with God, and tries to comfort himself with the thought that he will be vindicated by a latter-day kinsman who will take up his case. He concludes with a grim threat addressed to the friends.

19:2 *How long:* The opening of Job's reply echoes the opening of Bildad's speech.

19:3 *treated me coldly:* There is no agreement as to the meaning of the Hebrew word so translated, the etymology of which is unknown. I have translated it as if it were a variant of a similar-sounding root that means "alien," "strange," "unfamiliar," and that is sometimes used in connection with the unpleasant.

19:4 *does my fault wholly lie with me?:* The meaning is disputed. As translated, it means "even if I admit to having committed some slight wrongs, am I the only wrongdoer? You are doing a greater wrong by speaking to me so harshly, and God has done the greatest wrong by bringing all this suffering on me." Another possibility would be to translate this clause as declarative (i.e., "the fault lies with me") and to interpret it as "even if I admit to having committed some slight wrongs, they are known to me alone (so what right do you have to criticize me?)."

19:6 *got his net around me:* alluding back to Bildad's extended description of nets and snares as the punishment of the wicked, in the preceding chapter.

19:7 *"Violence!":* This expression seems to be the Bible's equivalent of our "Help! Murder!" Cf. Habakkuk 1:2.

19:17 *my own children:* literally, "the children of my belly." This phrase has vexed commentators ancient and modern, on the grounds that (1) as a man, Job cannot speak of "children of my belly"; and (2) Job's children cannot spurn their father on account of his disease, because according to the narrative they died before he was smitten, and therefore before the dialogue was supposed to have taken place. But "children of the belly" is an idiom used in the Bible with reference to men as well as women; cf. Deuteronomy 28:53 (the ancients correctly understood that children are as much the product of a man's body as they are of a woman's); and the death of Job's children in the narrative is only one of several inconsistencies between the narrative and the poem, some of which are more significant for the interpretation of the book. In any case, throughout the poem Job employs a stylized diction and set of images, some of which are known from other parts of the Bible, others not. We must never forget that Job is a literary work, not a transcript of real-life events; the author must have included many set pieces and passages of stylized rhetoric for his audience's pleasure, regardless of whether they made a perfect match with the frame.

19:20 *My bones cling to my skin and flesh:* This seems to be an expression for emaciation; a similar expression occurs in Psalms 102:6.

all I have left . . . teeth: This verse, as translated in the AV ("I am escaped with the skin of my teeth"), has become proverbial in English. Literal-minded modern commentators assign to the phrase "skin of my teeth" the clinical meaning of "gums." But it is simply an imaginative way of saying "nothing," and the sentence is similar in meaning to Job's earlier cry "Naked I came from my mother's womb/and naked I return there" (1:21). The meaning of the verb here translated as a verb of possession, however, is not completely clear in this context. The traditional "I have escaped"— the dictionary meaning of the verb—is also possible.

19:21 *the hand of a god has touched me:* Hebrew, unlike English, uses the expression "touched by God" to mean something bad, and possibly fatal. The root that underlies words meaning "touch" also underlies the word meaning "plague." I have chosen to preserve the word rather than to alter it to produce something more natural in English, like "struck," because I want the reader to see the same uncomfortable image that I do when I read this passage: of God's hand gently touching the body and leaving behind a wound that cannot heal.

19:23 copper: The Hebrew word looks like the ordinary one for "book" or "document," but the verb used with it and the parallelism with lead and rock suggest that Job is thinking of a material that is both hard and durable. Akkadian provides a word meaning "copper" that is almost identical to the Hebrew word used here. Rolls of copper and lead were used in antiquity as writing materials for documents that were meant to last, and have been discovered in the Middle East, as have monumental inscriptions on rock.

19:25 I know: It is almost impossible to read these lines without thinking of their Christological interpretation, so deeply ingrained is that interpretation in English, partly thanks to Handel's immortal aria "I Know That My Redeemer Liveth." But we have to try. Unfortunately, the text is full of difficulties; but when those words and expressions that do yield certain meaning are translated exactly, a train of thought emerges that can be made to fit the remainder without too much forcing.

Our starting point must be the Hebrew word *go'el*, the word traditionally rendered as "redeemer," and which I have rendered as "avenger." This word takes us back to a society composed of clans, in which close relatives, especially brothers, were responsible for obtaining justice or reestablishing stability for their kin by exacting blood vengeance in case they were murdered, purchasing their freedom if they were captured, or redeeming their property if it was sold for debt. Such a responsible kinsman is called the *go'el*. Biblical legislation tried to limit the practice of blood vengeance but made a principle out of the redemption of the person and property of kin. Both the word and the institution are mentioned frequently in biblical legislation and narrative. The word *go'el* played a central role in Israelite eschatology, which depicted God as responsible for Israel's well-being in the manner of a close relative; thus, God is called the redeemer of Israel, with special reference to His role as savior of His people from bondage in Egypt or from the later exile. From Jewish eschatology, the theme of redemption passed to Christianity, and the function of redeemer, to Christ, who is said to have redeemed the world from sin with his blood. But this later development is, of course, irrelevant to the Book of Job.

We are now in a better position to follow Job's thoughts. Though resigned to the fact that he will never have the face-to-face confrontation with God for which he has pleaded, Job has not abandoned the idea of a legal procedure that will show him to be in the right. If only his story could be written on imperishable materials, he feels quite certain that eventually an unknown kinsman will come forward, read the record, take up his case again, and gain the vindication he has been seeking, even though Job will not live to see it.

It is interesting again to watch Job struggling to formulate a solution that will permit a favorable outcome after this life has ended, yet failing to stumble on the idea of an afterlife, which a few hundred years later would become standard doctrine. In the long term, however, Job has been granted his vindication, for his document has been preserved, and we, his readers, share his outrage.

19:26–27 though . . . the thought: Unfortunately, at this emotional moment the text becomes opaque, and all translations of these verses are merely conjectures.

19:29 Shaddai's doom: Since there is no agreement on the meaning of the last word of this chapter, I have combined the two meanings attributed to it by different scholars into a single phrase.

Zophar's Second Speech

Zophar's second speech is entirely devoted to the fate of the wicked man, whose acquisitiveness is compared to gluttony. Images of food abound; the wicked man's food turns to poison in his belly, with grotesque and deadly results.

20:10 their hands will restore: Hebrew has "*his* hands." The point of the passage is that his heirs will have to make restitution after his death.

20:11 stuffed with his secret sin: The word translated here as "sin" normally means "youth," and many commentators understand it here to mean "youthful vigor." But it makes more sense to me to interpret it in the sense of its rare homonym, found also in Psalms 90:8. Well-being will be expressed in the very next chapter by the image of bones full of rich marrow (Job 21:24); this verse describes the wicked man as having bones full of sin.

20:18 *"Like the wealth, the return"*: The word translated as "return" simply cannot mean "trade," the interpretation adopted by most commentators. It means "replacement." The sentence's form recalls such proverbial expressions as "As the man, so is his strength" (Judg. 8:21). I understand it to be a commercial maxim meaning that a person gets out of an action or transaction what he puts into it. Here it is given a moral application: The wicked man gets the punishment to which his ill-gotten wealth entitles him.

20:22 *his measure:* i.e., his capacity for eating.

20:23 *rains down on him:* in Hebrew, "upon them."

20:24 *He flees the iron weapon:* The imagery seems to shift abruptly from the stomach pains suffered by the metaphorical glutton, i.e., the rapacious man, to a military attack against him. But by the end of the verse, it turns out that the military attack is itself a metaphor for the consequences of gluttony, a parenthetical metaphor within a larger metaphor.

the bow's bronze: i.e., a bronze-tipped arrow.

20:26 *All darkness is stored:* He faints, dimly conscious of the burning sensation in his belly. "Unfanned" means fanned by God, a ghastly, inhuman fire; for a similar expression, see 34:20.

20:27 *The heavens uncover his sin:* He vomits, revealing the wealth on which he has battened.

20:28 *uncovers the bounty inside his house:* Metaphorically, "his house" is the body of the glutton, i.e., the rapacious rich man. But the house also functions literally, as the place where he hides his ill-gotten wealth. The image and its meaning have become entangled in each other.

20:29 *This is what God . . . El:* similar wording to 27:13 and 31:2.

Job's Reply to Zophar's Second Speech

In the preceding speeches of the second round, which ends with this speech, the friends had devoted their speeches to depictions of the fate in store for the wicked. Job's response to Eliphaz was a mixture of attacks on his accusers and lament for his sufferings; his response to Bildad was focused completely on his suffering. Now responding to Zophar, Job at last takes up the substance of the three friends' speeches by stating boldly that the wicked do prosper, flatly contradicting their essential point and thereby raising the book's great moral question.

21:2 *let that be your act of consolation:* bitter sarcasm, and deserved, for in the second round, the friends had become so involved in their depictions of the fate of the wicked that they seem to have forgotten the purpose of their visit—to console Job for his suffering.

21:7 *grow old:* could also mean "grow rich." Compare Jeremiah's formulation of this question in Jeremiah 12:1–2.

21:13 *and all at once:* To die in the midst of prosperity and health is a blessing; cf. 5:26 and elsewhere in the book.

21:14–16 *Yet they had said to El . . . of the wicked!:* The wording is partly echoed by Eliphaz in his third speech, 22:17–18.

21:17 *How often . . . gutter:* The question contradicts Bildad's assertion in 18:5.

21:19–21 *Does God store up . . . determined?:* This passage contains, rather elliptically formulated, the following argument: If you say that God sometimes defers the punishment of the wicked man until the next generation, punishing his children for his sins, that is not right, for the wicked man himself is the one who should suffer. In the Hebrew text, the sinner is represented only by pronouns, obscuring the meaning. As interpreted here, the passage is a reply to Zophar's idea in 20:10 that the children of the wicked man might be the ones to make restitution for his extortions.

21:20 *his own doom:* emending an unintelligible word to one that is merely rare.

21:21 *has been determined:* The Hebrew word is difficult here, but the context dictates that it mean something like this. In 14:5, there was a similar—but, unfortunately, not identical—expression. The meaning of the Hebrew word seems to overlap with the ideas of the life span being determined and completed. No interpretation of this passage is acceptable that implies that the wicked man dies before his time, since the whole point is that the punishment is deferred until the next generation. That the dead man has no knowledge of or interest in the living was already pointed out by Job in 14:21.

21:22 *Does he teach knowledge to God . . . ?:* It is impossible to determine the function of this question within the context.

21:24 *his breasts full of milk:* I am not troubled by the femininity of this image, any more than I am by "the children of my belly" in 19:17. Some commentators who are troubled by it understand the word here translated as "breasts" to mean "jars." Others read the word meaning "milk" as "fat" (the two words are easily confused in Hebrew) and understand it to mean that his haunches are full of fat.

21:28 *"What has become of the nobleman's house?":* The word "nobleman" cannot, on lexical grounds, refer to the wicked, though many commentators have tried to interpret it that way in order to complete the parallelism between the two sentences. As the text stands, the "nobleman" must be Job himself. The house of the wicked is destroyed (as the friends have said several times—e.g., 18:21); Job's house has been destroyed; ergo, Job is one of the wicked. This is the claim of Job's opponents. Job now points out that this claim contradicts all experience.

21:31 *Who can reproach him . . . requite him?:* Does this verse refer to the all-powerful wicked man of the immediate context, or to God, the all-powerful deity of the larger context? The ambiguity is a bitter one.

21:32 *keeps watch over his mound:* Dhorme points out that tombs in Egypt and Palmyra are sometimes topped by a bust of the deceased, so that the dead man appears to be watching his own tomb. The word translated as "mound" ordinarily means a heap of sheaves, but presumably it can be used for a heap of earth as well.

The use of it here may be an ironic reference back to Eliphaz's speech in 5:26.

21:33 *sweet in his mouth:* This striking metaphor for the undeservedly tranquil eternal sleep of the wicked echoes and reverses Zophar's picture of the sweetness of evil under the wicked man's tongue in the preceding chapter (20:12ff.).

Eliphaz's Third Speech

Eliphaz's response to Job's complaint about the prosperity and complacency of the wicked is to put aside his former indirectness and accuse him of a list of specific crimes. He then tempers his attack by setting forth a rosy fantasy of the future that awaits Job if he changes his behavior and attitude.

22:2 *Is there anything:* The point of Eliphaz's opening lines is that, as he implied in his first speech, man is at best a most imperfect creature; Job should therefore not pretend to be completely righteous. Even if he were apparently so, it would mean little to the all-powerful deity.

do Him a favor: The pronoun in Hebrew is "them."

22:16 *men destroyed before time was:* The word translated as "destroyed" occurred in 16:8; since its exact meaning is unknown, my translation varies depending on the context in both places. The Hebrew phrase translated as "before time was" is usually understood to mean that they were destroyed before their time, and that is lexically possible; but in this context, the phrase seems to refer rather to the antiquity of events described, perhaps to some myth of primeval times. Eliphaz seems to be describing not the fate of the wicked in general, but that of a particular group of rebels against divine authority. Jewish tradition, sensing this implication of the passage but unaware of ancient Near Eastern mythology, interpreted it as referring to the story of the Flood. This idea is not far-fetched, but Eliphaz need not be thinking of the story of the Flood as recorded in Genesis, for other stories based on the same general motif were current in the ancient world. The reference could be to the myth of a primeval war among the gods, ending with the drowning of the rebel deities. The Hebrew word here translated as "flood," normally meaning "river," points in the direction of the ancient myths, for it is identical to the name of the Canaanite water deity Nahar.

22:17–18 *who said to El . . . of the wicked!:* The train of thought and some of the wording recall Job's speech in 21:14–16.

22:21 *Get close to Him:* Eliphaz opens the second part of his speech by playing on the two meanings of the verb he used at the beginning of the first part. There, it meant "to benefit."

22:24–25 *you will find ore . . . yours:* These two verses pose daunting philological problems; no translation can be more than an educated guess. But there is one thing they cannot mean, though some commentators and interpreters see it here: that Job should put aside materialistic concerns and devote himself to God. This ascetic view of piety is remote from the mentality of biblical religion. All three friends continually remind Job that if he behaves himself, he will be rewarded with riches. Wealth is considered a good thing in biblical religion, a mark of divine favor, though its possessors come in for much criticism.

22:24 *Ophir:* Though mentioned several times in the Bible as a source of gold, the site of Ophir has never been identified.

22:25 *god-size masses:* This translation is based on an interpretation found in some medieval Jewish commentaries.

22:27 *then you will fulfill your vows:* This is tantamount to saying that God will fulfill your wishes. It was a common practice to accompany a petitionary prayer with a vow to offer a sacrifice if the wish was fulfilled. Thus, "to fulfill a vow" means "to have a prayer answered." The psalms, many of which were originally liturgies accompanying sacrifices, contain references to such transactions between man and God—e.g., Psalm 116.

22:28 *Decree your bidding . . . :* Nearly all commentators, going back to the Talmud (Taanit 23a), take this to mean that Job will have the power to intercede on behalf of others.

22:29 *"Rise up!":* I am taking a word that is generally agreed to contain the root meaning of "height" to be a cry of encouragement.

22:30 *the guiltless man:* The Hebrew text requires a very slight emendation. As it stands, it means "the noninnocent." This reading would, however, contradict Eliphaz's point that the wicked must suffer. Fortunately, the word translated as "non" is only one letter short of the word for "man."

pure palms: (1) your innocence, which will give you the power to intercede successfully; (2) your palms, raised in supplication.

Job's Reply to Eliphaz's Third Speech

Eliphaz's attack does not divert Job from the theme of his preceding speech. After lamenting yet again that he cannot get a hearing from God, he depicts in detail the wickedness that goes unpunished in this world.

23:3 *If only I knew how to find Him:* In this version of Job's fantasy of a direct confrontation with God, he imagines that if he could achieve such a confrontation, God would give him the freedom to state his case without intimidation. But Job knows that God is inaccessible. By acknowledging that the confrontation will never take place, Job moves in the direction of accepting reality, a significant development in his emotional state.

23:6 *He would pay me close attention:* Another possible interpretation is, "He would help me."

23:8–9 *Forward I go . . . I cannot see:* In Hebrew, the four directions can signify the four cardinal points; accordingly, this passage could be translated as "east . . . west . . . north . . . south." But because Job wants to stress God's elusiveness, the smaller compass seems more appropriate here. The passage is a striking antithesis to the beautiful one in Psalms 139:8–9, in which the poet expresses gratitude to God for extending His providence to him whether he climbs to the heights, descends to the sea, or goes to the dawn (east) or the end of the sea (west). There, the larger compass is more appropriate to the context.

23:12 *more than my daily bread:* Rather than emend the Hebrew text, I have taken a Hebrew word that normally means "law" to mean "allotted portion," as in Proverbs 30:8 (the probable source of Jesus' "Give us this day our daily bread"). The word appears again later in the chapter (23:14).

23:13 *He is single-minded:* It is almost impossible to escape the force of the traditional Jewish interpretation of this verse, made familiar by the liturgy of Rosh Hashanah: that God acts as a single judge and does not share this function with or need the advice of anyone. But that interpretation does not fit this context. I take it to mean that when God focuses on a single desire, He pursues it unswervingly.

23:14 *what is allotted me:* presumably, of torments.

23:17 *for the dark has not yet cut me off:* I.e., since I am still alive, God has plenty more opportunities to torment me.

24:1 *Why are certain times . . . days?:* The verse is completely intelligible by itself, but its significance is obscure. The usual explanation is that the "times" and "days" are periods God sets aside for judging and punishing the wicked; Job asks why God does not have such fixed times set aside so that the wicked would be deterred from wrongdoing by the certainty of punishment.

familiars: presumably, soothsayers, men skilled at divining God's intentions, like Balaam, who is also said to be aware of God's intentions (Num. 24:16).

24:2 *They push back boundary markers:* i.e., the wicked.

24:3, 9 *take in pawn . . . take pledges:* In the simple rural society in the background of Job, where money was borrowed not for luxuries or investment but to hold off starvation, it was considered uncharitable to demand a pledge or interest for a loan; and it was considered particularly hard-hearted to take as a pledge the implements with which a person earned his living or the clothing from off his back. Some people must not have been ashamed to do so, for Deuteronomy tries to limit the practice through legislation; the same book prohibits the imposition of interest altogether.

24:5 *They live in the steppe . . . :* The lineation is designed to show that I see verses 5–8 and 10–11 as describing the hard life of the simple poor who are exploited by the wicked rich. But other interpretations of the passage are possible.

24:11 *within rich men's walls:* literally, "between their walls," with the referent of the pronoun unspecified. Presumably, it refers to the walls of the rich man's olive orchards, where the poor laborers are virtually imprisoned; or "between their rows," i.e., rows of olive trees.

24:12 *they die:* The Hebrew text uses a rare Hebrew word for "people," a word that also happens to resemble the ordinary participle meaning "dying."

24:13 *Here are some of those . . . :* The people who "defy the light" depicted in this passage are three classes of criminals—murderers, adulterers, and housebreakers (an interesting correspondence with the six, seventh, and eighth of the Ten Commandments)—who are perversely more comfortable with night than with day. The opening sentence of this passage almost sounds as if it could be another reference to a creation myth, but no myth has been identified in which the rebel gods are portrayed as rebels against the light. Accordingly, I have translated it in the present tense.

24:14 I have taken the liberty of shifting the third clause of verse 14 (literally, "At night he is like a thief") to the beginning of verse 16.

    evening: The word used here normally means "light" in biblical Hebrew, which would suggest dawn. I have interpreted it in accordance with the use of the word in Hebrew of a slightly later period and its cognate in Aramaic, as demanded by the context.

24:17 *morning is deathdark:* They fear morning the way others fear deathdark, but they are familiar with deathdark and comfortable with it.

24:18–24 *By day they flee lightly . . . corn:* This passage is one of the longest stretches of barely intelligible text in the book. Many of its clauses make sense in themselves but do not fit the preceding and following clauses, so that it is very hard even to get the drift of the meaning. Much of this passage seems better suited to the hypothetical third speech of Zophar, which many scholars see as being hidden in chapter 27. The translator has two choices: to follow the practice of academic scholarship and move it, piece by piece, to other sections of the book, at the same time emending it heavily; or to work it with a lot of imagination and try to make it fit. There are arguments in favor of both approaches. Although in the course of the translation I have allowed myself the liberty of occasionally emending or relocating a verse or a phrase, I cannot reconcile myself to such large-scale changes unless they are completely convincing and unless the reason for the original dislocation can easily be explained.

The solution I have adopted is to translate this passage in accordance with the imaginative interpretation of a medieval Provençal commentator, Rabbi Levi ben Gerson (1288–1344). This reading is at least internally consistent and is hardly less plausible than those proposed by the moderns. To satisfy the curiosity of the reader who wishes to see just how much Levi ben Gerson's interpretation adds to the literal meaning of the Hebrew text in order to arrive at a coherent interpretation, here, for comparison's sake, is a close translation of the Hebrew:

> Light he is on the surface of waters;
>> their plot of land is cursed;
>> he does not turn by way of vineyards.
> Desert and heat steal waters of snow;
>> they sinned in Sheol.
> The womb forgets him;
>> the worm finds him sweet;
>> he is remembered no more.
>> Wickedness is broken like a tree.
> He treats the barren woman harshly, she does not bear;
>> he gives no help to the widow.
> He draws mighty ones with his strength,
>> he rises, but is not secure of his life.
> He gives him for security and he leans,
>> and his eyes are on their paths.
> They are elevated for a while and are no more;
>> they are crushed down; like all, they are compressed;
>> they wither like the top of a wheat stalk.

Bildad's Third Speech

Bildad begins an impressive speech describing the might of the creator. He seems to intend to reduce the tension of the debate by shifting the focus from Job's supposed wickedness to that of man in general. But his eloquence is truncated. We might imagine Job impatiently interrupting him, breaking in to deliver a speech of his own along the same lines. Many modern scholars believe, however, that the part of chapter 26 (26:5–14) that describes the creator's might is actually a displaced continuation of Bildad's speech.

25:5–6 *Even the moon . . . even the stars. . . . What then . . . :* Eliphaz used similar rhetoric in 4:17–18 and 15:14–16.

Job's Reply to Bildad's Third Speech

Job impatiently breaks off Bildad's speech. He is just as aware of God's might as is Bildad, and can speak of it at least as eloquently.

26:5 *Shades:* the shadowy spirits of the dead. The underworld is sometimes imagined as being not merely under the earth but under the water that is beneath the earth (Ps. 136:6).

their inhabitants: the mysterious aquatic creatures of the deep ocean.

26:6 *Abaddon:* another name for the underworld. The word means "perishing."

26:7 *Mount Zaphon:* the Hebrew name of a mountain celebrated in Semitic myths as the sacred mountain of Baal, identified by scholars as Jebel al-Aqra in Syria. The Hebrew word for "north" is derived from this name.

chaos: the unformed matter of which the world was created (Gen. 1:2), the thought of which caused ancient man anxiety.

26:9 *Throne:* probably refers to the sky. The sky is pictured as God's throne in Exodus 24:10; cf. Isaiah 66:1. The theme of God's throne was to play an important part in later Jewish mysticism.

26:12 *Yamm . . . Rahab:* the primeval ocean, personified as a god, and the ocean monster of Canaanite myth; both have already been referred to several times.

26:13 *in a net:* This formerly obscure verse is rendered perfectly clear by a passage in the Mesopotamian creation epic. In this work, written in Akkadian, the creator-god Marduk uses both wind and a net to ensnare the sea monster. The Akkadian word for "net" is practically identical to a word in our verse.

26:14 *gaze:* literally, "contemplate." What Job has just related is only a vague rumor, and it is terrifying enough. Who could tolerate the actual experience of such a puissant deity? Yet that is just what Job had been asking for in his earlier speeches, and this passage eerily anticipates the denouement, when Yahweh actually does appear in chapter 38.

Job's Last Word to His Friends

The expected third speech by Zophar and third reply by Job do not exist in the book's present form. There is no way to tell if they have been lost or were never written. As the book now stands, it appears that Job, unable to convince his friends of his innocence, explodes at them in rage. His opening words in this speech, the closest he comes to blasphemy in all the book, make it clear that he is at the end of his rope.

After calling God as his witness and insisting on the rightness of his position and of his conduct, he now calls down imprecations on his friends. For the rest of the chapter, he describes the dreadful fate of the wicked *in the friends' own terms,* praying that all the disasters they believe are in store for the wicked fall upon them. This interpretation of the chapter necessitates taking Job's imprecations as ironic, a procedure that allows him full scope to vent his rage, and a use of language that I find psychologically plausible.

But readers who are troubled by Job's seeming to take the position of his opponents so eloquently (since he has fiercely maintained that the wicked never get their deserts) cannot accept the ironic interpretation of the chapter. To solve this problem, it has been proposed that the part of chapter 27 in which Job seems to be adopting the friends' view, verses 8–23, is actually Zophar's missing third speech. The formula "Zophar the Naamatite answered" has, in this view, fallen out before verse 8. To the balance of the chapter, some add the obscure passage from 24:18 to 24:25. But these adjustments still do not provide a reply by Job to Zophar's putative third speech, so that the dialogue would still remain incomplete. I therefore think that, unless a more coherent ancient version of Job turns up, the explanation of the sequence of ideas given above is at least as convincing as the assumption that the chapters of the book have somehow been misarranged.

27:7 *my enemy . . . my opponent:* i.e., the friends.

27:13 *Here is what God . . . Shaddai:* almost the same words as at the end of Zophar's second speech in 20:29. The repetition could be evidence in favor of viewing this part of the chapter as Zophar's missing third speech; or it could be justified as an ironic quotation by Job of his opponents' own words.

27:15 *widows:* The plural fits the social reality, since polygamy was common, especially among the wealthy.

A Meditation on Wisdom

After the intensity of the dialogue between Job and his friends, we come to a quieter passage in the voice of an omniscient speaker rather than in that of any of the participants in the dialogue. Perhaps the author thought the reader needed an interlude before being confronted with Job's final passionate speeches.

The theme of wisdom is actually quite relevant to the subject matter of the book. The friends represent standard ancient wisdom, and it is this world view that Job has been objecting to all along. In the poem's denouement, Yahweh will appear and denounce human pretensions to understanding the wisdom of his management of the universe. The Meditation on Wisdom anticipates this very point, but in a serene tone rather than in the dramatic one of Yahweh speaking from the storm. When we encounter the Meditation here, we may not grasp its importance in the scheme of the book. But after reading chapters 38–41, we realize retroactively that its purpose is to prepare us for the book's conclusion.

The Meditation is in two parts and is organized in such a way as to keep the reader in the dark for a while about where it is headed. It begins with an encomium on man, praising his enterprise and ingenuity in seeking out precious minerals in the most out-of-the-way and dangerous places. The passage is so appreciative of man as a doer and thinker that it might well have come from a Greek drama. (It specifically recalls the chorus in Sophocles' *Antigone*, lines 332–72; let us remember that the classic Greek tragedies could well be contemporaneous with Job!) The contrasting second part says that all of man's devices are not adequate for the mining of divine wisdom, which is hidden far more profoundly than material treasures. How, then, can man achieve wisdom? The answer, kept back till the very last verse, is that wisdom is completely inaccessible to man. Man can only fear and revere the Lord, who created all things and who alone can find wisdom. For a creature as imperfect as man, piety is wisdom; but wisdom itself lies only with God.

28:3 *He puts an end to darkness:* The implied subject is man.

28:11 *nether sources:* based on a slight emendation.

28:13 *No man knows how to reach it:* based on the emendation of one letter.

28:16–19 *It cannot be valued . . . purest gold:* This passage employs no fewer than four different words for gold, whereas English has only one, posing a problem for the translator similar to that of the lions in 4:10–11.

28:16 *Ophir:* See note to 22:24.

28:18 *Wisdom is better than bags of rubies:* literally, "A bag of wisdom is better than rubies."

28:22 *Abbadon* is the underworld (see above, note to 26:6); *Mot,* its deity (see above, note to 18:13).

28:27 *examined it:* based on a minuscule emendation.

Job Reviews His Condition Past and Present

The interlude on wisdom over, Job now delivers a long and passionate speech lamenting how his social position has been compromised by his suffering. The speech is in two parts, the first describing his former power and prestige, and the second, the taunts that he has had to endure from the outcasts of society. He concludes with a final complaint about God and a burst of self-pity.

29:4 *protecting:* This reading, which recalls the Accuser's description (1:10) of Job's special status, is obtained by altering a single letter.

29:7 *When I would stride out . . . :* Here begins a remarkably vivid and extended picture of public life in an ancient town and the status of the town's great man.

29:18 *live as long as the phoenix:* literally, "I shall multiply days like sand." Sand is commonly used in hyperbolic similes expressing the concept of innumerability, e.g., "I shall multiply your seed like the sand on the seashore" (Gen. 22:17). I have followed the more colorful (though philologically uncertain) interpretation of the Jewish tradition. The phoenix, a fabulous bird in Egyptian and Greek lore, is said to live for hundreds of years, then burn itself to death in its nest, from which a new phoenix arises.

29:20 *my bow blooming in my hand:* The bow returns to its natural state and sprouts as if it had never been cut from the tree, perhaps an image of continued virility. (For the bow as an emblem of virility, see the Babylonian Talmud, Sota 36b.)

29:21 *They would listen . . . waiting:* as we too have been waiting for Job to pick up the colorful description of his audience in the town square, from which he had digressed, lost in satisfied recollection of his acts of charity. By this rhetorical maneuver, the author makes it seem as if the street scene had been briefly frozen and that it resumes its motion here.

29:24 *When I smiled at them:* When Job would smile at petitioners, they would fear his smile would not last and would take care to continue to please him.

29:26 *like one who comforts men who mourn:* It would appear from a number of passages in Job that comforting mourners was a special responsibility of a dignitary. There is therefore a certain similarity between a king among his troops and a comforter among mourners; in each case, the great man appears and makes an address, while everyone present listens in hushed respect.

30:1 *And now . . . :* The characteristic parallelism of Hebrew poetry is noticeably absent from this verse. The unexpected breakdown of literary discipline is a striking signal of the shift to the contrasting theme. The description that follows of the marginal people living outside civilization is one of the most remarkable passages in the book.

30:4 *to get warm:* This translation necessitates changing the vowels of the Hebrew word.

30:5 *from society:* literally, "from inside."

30:11 *undid my cord:* For this idiom, see 12:18.

30:12 *Young bullies:* The bastard children of the outlaws grow up away from civilization and run free, spreading chaos.

  range anywhere: literally, "they send their foot free," an expression associated with grazing animals irresponsibly set free to graze anywhere, with destructive results. The Hebrew text reads "*my* foot."

30:18 *Just to dress . . . my waist:* This paraphrase reflects the interpretation of this obscure verse by Saadiah Gaon. "My collar fits my waist" means he is emaciated.

30:19 *He conceived me as clay,/and I have come to be like dust and ashes:* Cf. 10:9 for the same idea.

30:22 *You lift me up . . . cunning:* This image may be an ironic use of the language of theophany, since Yahweh is often described as appearing mounted on a wind or storm (e.g., Ps. 18:11); or of prophecy, since the prophet Ezekiel is lifted up on a wind when he sees God (Ezek. 3:14). But Job is mounted on a destructive wind that renders him helpless, like the wicked man at the end of chapter 27. This image and the one in the following verse form a merism, a pair of images of opposite extremes—in this case, of high and low.

30:29 *jackal's brother:* i.e., constantly howling. The jackal and the ostrich regularly serve as images for wailing and mourning in biblical poetry.

Job's Oath

Job began by cursing his day and concludes with an oath. In the course of the exchange of speeches with the friends, he has made emotional progress, moving from despair to defiance.

The oath was a judicial procedure, a kind of conditional curse on oneself, in the form: "If I have done *x*, then may *y* befall me." The terrifying consequences were often designed to be in some way parallel to the crime; this chapter provides several examples. On the rhetorical level, this chapter also reflects the common practice of omitting the "then" clause, it being understood that if the speaker has committed the specified acts, he wishes a dreadful doom of an unspecified kind upon himself. The oath was considered probatory, but since it was greatly feared, it was sparingly employed. Job's use of it here is a last resort to convince his friends of his innocence. But it is also directed at God, who has refused to exchange words with Job, a unilateral technique to compel Him to set Himself right by vindicating Job.

The first verse of chapter 31 ("I have made a pact with my eyes / never to gaze at young women") seems to be misplaced, but different readers have suggested different places for it. I have moved it to the position following verse 12. Irrespective of whether this verse is left at the head of the chapter or moved, the speech opens rather abruptly, as if it is a continuation of something that has been lost.

31:2 *Then what does . . . have in store:* Though couched as a question, the phrasing recalls 20:29 and 27:13.

31:4 *count all my steps:* The theme of counting one's steps recurs toward the end of the chapter (31:37).

31:10 *may my own wife grind for another:* This is often interpreted as a metaphor for sexual exploitation, like the image in the next line. But grinding is often mentioned in the Bible as an image of servitude, as in Lamentations 5:13. There really isn't much difference, as a slave woman would be used for both heavy work and sex.

31:12 *For it:* adultery.

Abbadon: the underworld, as in 28:22.

31:14 *when God comes forward:* The eschatological theme of God's eventually coming to demand a reckoning seems out of place in Job. Perhaps it is a way of expressing the idea of individual conscience, which is merely inchoate in the Bible.

31:18 *for since . . . guided her:* These hyperboles simply mean that Job has been concerned with the plight of the orphan all his life. The images of his own youth are intended to reflect his lifelong empathy with the young and helpless, not literally to date the beginning of his concern.

31:21 *If ever I raised my hand . . . in the gate:* As often in the Bible, "the gate" is equivalent to "the street," or "the town square," the site of commercial and judicial activity in ancient towns. In chapters 29–30, we saw Job himself administering justice in the street. This passage is generally understood to mean that Job never took advantage of the helpless when he saw that the street or the tribunal was full of his own supporters.

31:27 *and my hand . . . my mouth:* to kiss one's hand while looking at someone or to waft a kiss in his direction is a sign of adoration. Pope refers to a Babylonian statue representing a worshiper making this gesture to a god. In this passage, in which Job speaks about being seduced by the sun and the moon, the image has a decidedly erotic ring, as references to the idolatrous worship of astral phenomena often have in the Bible. The sensitivity of the subject matter is underscored by the coy way in which the crime is described.

Even more than the naming of Yahweh in 12:9, this reference to idolatry as a crime is a notable intrusion of the Israelite religious sensibility in a book that generally avoids issues associated with Israel's peculiar covenant theology. Yet Yahweh is not named here. The designation of the deity in the passage "for it would mean denying God on high" is not Yahweh but El. Because of the strongly monotheistic tone of this passage, I have not left it as El—my usual practice—but replaced it with God.

31:30 *execration:* a formal, ritualistic curse.

31:31 *If the men of my household . . . flesh:* This translation represents exactly (but in idiomatic English) the lexical meaning of the sentence.

31:34 *kept silent . . . outdoors:* This passage creates the impression that in Job's world, merely keeping to oneself is a kind of wrongdoing, or at least arouses suspicion of wrongdoing. Job is not confessing to any particular crime here, only saying that his not withdrawing from society is evidence of his blamelessness. It is as if privateness itself is perceived as a misdemeanor, an uncomfortable truth at all times.

31:35–37 *If only I had someone to hear me . . . as before a prince:* I have split verse 40 into two parts and moved this passage into the space between them, to produce a more natural peroration. In the Hebrew text, this passage occurs before "If my land cries out because of me . . . barley" (31:38–40), interrupting Job's oath.

In the concluding words of his final speech, Job reiterates for the last time his wish that he could at least be informed as to what he is accused of. The writ of indictment itself would be a thing he could bear with pride, and it would enable him to defend himself fairly. The peroration is rhetorically linked to the body of the oath by the conditional form of expression.

31:35 *my desire:* based on a small emendation.

Elihu Speaks

The dialogue concluded, we are unexpectedly presented with a new character, Elihu. The narrator explains that Elihu is a younger man who has been following the debate with mounting dissatisfaction, and who now comes forward to present his own views on Job's problems. Elihu delivers four addresses, but no reply by the other speakers is reported.

Though long-winded compared with the other speakers, Elihu does add one or two new ideas to the discussion, as well as some excellent poetry. In his first speech, he raises the new idea of a supernatural intercessor who might help Job, contradicting Eliphaz's statement that there are no intercessors who are in a position to help. In his fourth speech, he gives an elaborate picture of God's control of the weather as evidence of His supreme wisdom and power. This speech, especially the description of the storm in chapter 37, is thought by many scholars to anticipate the speeches of Yahweh in chapters 38—41 and render them anticlimactic. Furthermore, Elihu's speeches seem to disrupt the logical structure of the book, for it is odd that a new character is introduced when the structure of the book has prepared the reader for the denouement. For these reasons, most scholars agree that these six chapters were added to the book by a later writer.

Elihu's first speech is in two parts, corresponding to the chapter division. He begins by explaining that he has chosen not to speak until now out of deference to his seniors; but since the older men have talked themselves out to no avail, he feels free to enter the discussion and speak frankly, sparing no one's feelings. In the second part, which is addressed to Job, he attacks Job for insisting that he is innocent and God capricious. God makes men suffer as a warning and restores them if they repent. This cycle may recur several times. But such salvation often depends on an intercessor who induces God to give the person another chance.

32:3 *making God appear to be in the wrong:* The Hebrew text has "Job" instead of "God," a typical avoidance of blasphemy, similar to the use of "curse" instead of "bless" in the narrative of chapters 1—2.

32:9 *Elders are not always wise . . . :* The Hebrew text translated literally means, "Elders are not wise, and the old do not understand judgment." This statement is so contrary to the common wisdom of the ancient world, the repeatedly expressed opinion of biblical authors, and Elihu's elaborate attempts at courtesy that I, like some other commentators, have felt constrained to soften it.

32:12 *no one has refuted Job:* Elihu is the only one of the disputants to refer to Job by name, and he does so repeatedly.

32:13 *"Now we have met true wisdom . . .":* I.e., you should not break off the argument thinking that in Job you have found divine wisdom.

32:15–22 *Intimidated . . . carry me off:* If Elihu is addressing these lines to himself, it is an unparalleled case in Job of an extended internal monologue. It is also possible that with these words, he turns away from the friends and addresses Job.

32:19 *unopened wine:* i.e., like a tightly sealed leather wine jar swollen with the gas produced by fermentation. The image of flatulence reinforces the impression of Elihu as brash and uncultivated.

32:22 *my maker would soon carry me off:* generally interpreted to mean that if Elihu resorted to euphemisms or indirect speech, God would punish him with sudden death.

33:4 *El's spirit . . . Shaddai's breath:* This is the source of his wisdom, the thing sometimes lacking in elders, as Elihu said in 32:8.

33:6 *pinched:* This verb is an interesting link to ancient Babylonian myths, which use it to describe both the action of a potter and the fashioning of man by a god.

33:7 *no compulsion:* Elihu is alluding to Job's own words in 9:34 and 13:21, where Job had protested that he could not argue his case effectively before God because of God's intimidating presence. The Hebrew word here translated as "compulsion" reinforces the allusion to 13:21, because it sounds like "palm" in that verse.

33:11 *He puts my feet in stocks:* Job's own language in 13:27.

33:15 *In a dream . . . :* Eliphaz's language in 4:13.

33:16 *and frightens them:* emending the vocalization.

33:18 *the Death Canal:* The word used here and in 36:12, formerly understood to refer to a kind of weapon, is now known to mean "a pool" or "a channel"; the reference is to the river of hell, known as "Hubur" in Mesopotamian mythology and "Styx" in Greek.

33:22 *the Killers:* Although infernal demons do not occur elsewhere in the Bible, they do appear in Akkadian and later Jewish literature.

33:23–24 *but if . . . character:* The idea of the intercessor is a late-appearing theme in the book. As stated here, it seems to mean that while most people sin and suffer for it, a person may occasionally be saved by the intercession of an angel. But in the course of the speech, the saving agent seems more like a friend who effectively counsels the sufferer to shun his evil ways, i.e., someone like Elihu himself.

33:26 *He appeals to a god . . . :* Another new theme introduced by Elihu late in the book: The penitent can dream not only of material restoration but of satisfaction at being restored to divine favor. This may be a glimmering of what we would call spiritual satisfaction. This fantasy in which the penitent gives public testimony to his restoration to divine favor is supported by several of the psalms (e.g., Ps. 118), which may actually have served the cultic function of individual thanksgiving envisioned here.

33:28 *to enjoy the light:* literally, "to see the light," which in Hebrew does not mean "to suddenly achieve understanding," as in English, but "to live."

Elihu's Second Speech

Elihu's second speech is punctuated by appeals to men of intelligence, implying that Job, by his words, has shown that he does not belong in that category. He denounces Job for accusing God of injustice, and points out that although the wicked may appear to prosper, their fall often occurs unexpectedly.

34:3 *The ear is the best judge of speech . . . tasty:* same phrase as in 12:11.

34:5 *the god denies me justice:* similar phrase to 27:2.

34:23 *For El does not set man a certain date:* describing the uncertainty of an individual's life span. In 24:1, Job had complained that God does not set fixed times for judging the wicked.

34:30 *Better . . . people:* The sentence is fragmentary in the Hebrew.

34:33 *you reject His judgment?:* The last two words are not in the Hebrew. Every translation and commentary proposes a different solution to the problems posed by this verse.

34:37 *slaps his hands:* a gesture of mourning; Elihu is criticizing Job for wailing and lamenting over his own suffering. By so doing, he is adding to his original sin the act of rebellion against God's judgment.

Elihu's Third Speech

In this, the shortest of Elihu's four speeches, he berates Job for thinking that God does not see wrongdoing. God is too lofty to be affected by man's behavior, whether good or wicked; therefore, He does not respond immediately to man's misbehavior or his suffering. But that does not mean that He is unaware. A person should do good and bear suffering in silence and wait for God to take action in His own good time.

35:5 Look up: echoes Eliphaz in 22:12–14.

35:6 If you do sin: Elihu turns Job's question around: Job had asked what benefit he gets from being good, what harm from doing wrong. Elihu wants him to ask what benefit God gets from Job's good behavior or what harm from his bad behavior. God cannot be affected, only Job can; therefore, it behooves him to watch his step.

35:8 Your wrongs . . . like you: I.e., a person's good or bad behavior affects only himself.

35:10 who grants us song by night: The meaning of this memorable phrase is contested. There is good reason for taking the word translated as "song" to mean something within the semantic range of "strength." Doing so would dictate a completely different interpretation of the passage as a whole from the one given here. But I have adopted the more familiar explanation of the word because I cannot think of a convincing interpretation of the passage based on this other explanation. I understand the verse to mean that the oppressed, like Job, cry out against God in their suffering, forgetting that God often gives them pleasure as well as pain.

35:11 who makes us wiser . . . birds of heaven: It is a commonplace of ancient wisdom literature that man can learn the profound lessons of life by observing nature. (A familiar example is Jesus' parable beginning, "Behold the fowls of the air," Matt. 6:26.) The lesson here is that man should bear the troubles of life patiently, like the animals. Yahweh Himself will provide a spectacular example of the kind of wisdom to be gotten from nature in His speech from the storm, chapters 38–41.

35:15 *since he has chosen otherwise:* Elihu has abruptly shifted from his main theme back to Job's state of mind, speaking of him in the third person, as if he has turned to the two friends. The translation of this verse is conjectural.

Elihu's Fourth Speech

Elihu's fourth and longest speech is in two parts, with the division marked by the introductory word "Behold!" In the first part (36:5–21), he goes over familiar ground, reiterating the themes of God's justice that he and the three friends have already thoroughly rehearsed, and urging Job to mend his ways. In the second (36:22–37:24), he speaks of God's power over nature, describing in impressive poetic detail the coming of a thunderstorm, its clearing-off, and its replacement by hot weather.

36:5 *does not reject a man for nothing:* Hebrew text has only "does not reject"; I have translated this as if it were a shortened version of "God would not reject the innocent" in 8:20.

36:10 *and tells them to repent their sin:* literally, "return." Surprisingly, this is the only definite occurrence in the entire book of this word with this meaning, which is so common in the prophetic writings and in Hebrew religious writing generally. In 22:23, where the same Hebrew verb occurred, the nuance of repentance was marked explicitly by the addition of the words "to God."

36:12 *the Death Canal:* See 33:18.

    and die unwitting: i.e., without having learned their lesson; or perhaps it means that they die without even realizing what is happening to them, as in 4:20 (". . . perish forever, not even aware of their fate").

36:13 *cry out:* i.e., appeal to God for help.

36:14 *live out their lives among the holy shades:* The text has "cultic prostitutes," which, despite the ingenuity of exegetes, cannot be correct. Altering one vowel mark results in the reading "holy ones." The dead were considered divine in Egyptian religion; the same may have been true in ancient Israel, for when

Samuel's shade returns to the earth, the Witch of Endor exclaims that she sees a divinity arising from the earth (1 Sam. 28:13).

36:15 *He releases . . . through hardship:* The suffering of the sufferer is intended to purify him and induce him to change his ways.

36:16–21 *Take you . . . rather than that!:* very obscure verses, yielding very different meanings to different interpreters. "With Him" reflects a slight emendation.

36:22 *Behold!:* This word, which introduces the second part of Elihu's speech, also occurs at the beginning of verses 26 and 30, linking these verses, which are a kind of preamble to the lengthy description, beginning in verse 30, of God's power as revealed in storms. The word "sublime" has a similar unifying function; I have used this word to translate three Hebrew words of similar sound and related meaning occurring in verses 22, 24, and 26, and a fourth time at the end of Elihu's speech, 37:23.

36:24 *at which all mankind gazes:* The verb is usually translated as "sung," which does not seem to fit the context as well as the admittedly much rarer usage resorted to here.

36:26 *Behold! El, sublime beyond . . . numbering:* an echo of 5:9 and 9:10.

36:27 *fog:* Good evidence exists that the word so translated actually refers to the body of water that ancient peoples thought underlay the earth, alluded to several times already in Job. Nevertheless, I have retained the traditional explanation of the word, as better suited to the context.

36:29 *His pavilion:* El's pavilion (Hebrew: *sukka*) refers to a hutlike grouping of dark clouds that the ancient imagination saw as sheltering the storm deity. The expression occurs several times in Psalms.

36:30 *lightning:* literally, light. A surprising feature of Elihu's description of the storm is that he never uses the ordinary Hebrew word for "lightning," but four times uses the word for "light" instead. In the following verses (except for verses 11 and 15), I translate accordingly without further comment. See also 38:24.

over the clouds: Hebrew text reads "over it."

NOTES

36:31 *He dooms some nations:* El judges nations by punishing them with lightning or rewarding them with abundant rain.

36:32 *fills His palms:* The Hebrew text says that He "covers" His palms with lightning, meaning that El's palms, here a metaphor for "clouds," are briefly obliterated by the flash of lightning. Clouds are compared to palms in 1 Kings 18:44.

directs it with sure aim: adopted verbatim from Pope's commentary.

36:33 *of His furious rage against evil:* All translations of this obscure phrase are mere guesswork.

37:4 *no one can trace its path:* I.e., the lightning and thunder disappear without a trace.

37:5 *makes things great . . . knowing:* yet another echo of 5:9 and 9:10.

37:7 *He seals up:* during the winter, like Noah during the Flood. This translation necessitates two small emendations.

37:9 *Then from its chamber:* chambers in which meteorological phenomena are stored until needed; see 9:9 and 38:22.

scatter-wind: Pope's translation of a unique Hebrew word, based on the medieval commentaries and modern etymological analysis. Traditionally, the word has been understood to be a variant of "constellations," which would also be acceptable, since prescientific peoples believed that the weather depended on astral influences.

37:11 *But then He drives off:* My interpretation of this difficult verse is loosely based on the ancient Aramaic version.

37:13 *whether for the rod . . . :* The verse mentions three levels: "for the rod," i.e., extremes of weather to punish the earth; "sufficiency," i.e., adequate weather; and "grace," i.e., perfect weather conditions, a sign of particular blessing. But "sufficiency" results from a slight emendation to the text.

37:18 *solid as a brazen mirror:* Mirrors in antiquity were made of polished metal.

37:21 *has made them glow:* At first glance, the verb seems to mean "purifies them." But it could have the meaning of the equivalent root in Aramaic (also found in Hebrew in Exod. 24:10), which would yield this translation.

37:23 *He will never answer*: The text, as vocalized, reads, "He does not torment." The translation is based on a slight emendation of the vowel markings added to the Hebrew text in the Middle Ages. The resulting reading yields a conclusion to Elihu's speech that is much more appropriate to the structure of the book and consonant with the conclusion of chapter 28, the Meditation on Wisdom. It also lends irony to Yahweh's intervention in the verse after next (38:1). If the traditional vocalization is maintained, it would be possible to translate: ". . . sublime in power and great in justice; he would not torment," which is perfectly acceptable, but considerably less charged.

37:24 *Therefore, mortals, fear Him . . . cannot see*: This interpretation, based on an untranslatable pun in the Hebrew, is unusual, though it is mentioned as a possibility by one of the medieval commentators.

Yahweh's Reply to Job

All speakers now having fallen silent, Yahweh appears in a storm, His usual manifestation in the Bible. In an address of tremendous eloquence and vigor, He describes how He founded the earth, bound the seas inside their proper limits, arranged the luminaries, organized the world's weather, and saw to the sustenance of the various animals and birds. The point is that Job, a mere human being, is incapable of doing these things or even of knowing how they were done; the implication is that he is therefore incapable of understanding the meaning of his suffering or even of his own life. The force of God's answer stuns Job. In two laconic lines of Hebrew verse, he acknowledges that he has no response and undertakes to be silent.

Yahweh's description of His activities as the creator and sustainer of the world is couched in a series of vignettes, each devoted to a particular natural phenomenon or animal species. (None of the vignettes is devoted to man.) The first few of these, dealing with the luminaries and the ocean, recall the ancient myths that have already been alluded to several times in Job and that are referred to elsewhere in the Bible; thus, while beautifully phrased, they cover ground that is fairly familiar by now. But the animal descriptions are quite original. One after the other, the fauna of Job's world—ibis, lion, antelope, wild ass, buffalo, ostrich, horse, and vulture—are paraded before us, as they were before the first man (Gen. 2:19). In treating the first few of these, the poem continues to subordinate the description to the theme of Yahweh's providence and Job's ignorance. The form is: "Who gave wisdom to the ibis?" or "Do you hunt prey for the lioness?" "Do you know when the antelope gives birth?" "Who gave the wild ass his freedom?" But sarcasm soon gives way to description for its own sake, and by the time we reach the ostrich, the poet has put the didactic framework completely aside in order to indulge himself—and us—in pure nature poetry.

38:7 *when the morning stars were all singing:* The stars are imagined as lesser gods, members of Yahweh's court or army. As such, they hailed His feat in establishing the world. Psalm 148 also describes the stars, along with all the other features of the universe, as singing Yahweh's praises.

38:8–11 *Who barred the sea . . . breakers' surge:* Several of the details of this passage have parallels in Ugaritic and Akkadian creation myths.

38:13 *and shake the wicked out of it:* This moral aside is unique in the chapter and a bit of a puzzle. Most likely it is part of the mythic creation motif. The "wicked" are the forces of nature that Yahweh vanquished at the beginning of the world. Another possible solution may be found in the domain of human society: The "wicked" are ordinary human criminals who perpetrate their wicked deeds at night and fear exposure by day, as described in 24:13–17.

38:14 *They stand up naked:* emending "like a garment" to "without a garment."

38:24 *where lightning forks:* taking the Hebrew word for "light" to mean "lightning," as in Elihu's speeches. See the note to 36:30.

38:36 *ibis . . . cock:* Both words are obscure. For the reasoning behind the rendering "ibis," see Dhorme's commentary to this verse. "Cock" is the interpretation of Jewish tradition.

40:5 One time . . . two times: This type of poetic formula has been commented upon several times already; cf. the note to 33:14.

Yahweh's Reply to Job Continued

Yahweh begins His second speech with the sarcastic demand that Job defend himself and demonstrate his right and power to challenge Yahweh as he has done. Then Yahweh goes on to describe two more beasts, ostensibly continuing the series of animal descriptions that broke off at the end of chapter 39. But the descriptions that make up the body of this second speech are different in character from those in chapters 38–39. The first of the two beasts is not named but is simply called *behemot* ("animals," but construed as a singular noun; this Hebrew word is the source of the English word "behemoth"), here rendered as "the River Beast." The second is called by the mythological term *livyatan* (Leviathan), represented in this translation by "the River Coiler," which is partly based on the word's presumed etymology. For the mythological associations of Leviathan, see the note to 3:8. While some of the two beasts' features are naturalistic, other features are more extreme than what can be observed in ordinary nature. The amount of space devoted to them, especially to the River Coiler, is much greater than that devoted to any of the animals described in Yahweh's first speech. Finally, while the creatures of Yahweh's first speech are creatures of land and sky, both the creatures of the second speech are associated with water, the element frequently mentioned in mythology as the realm of chaos that the great god had to bring under control before He could create the world; yet they are not fish. They are thus creatures of undetermined, liminal, and therefore mysterious character. In all these ways, the description of these two beasts contrasts markedly with those in the preceding chapters, in which even the lion, the most redoubtable of land animals, is treated merely as one of the crowd of varied creatures familiar to observation. The two creatures of Yahweh's second speech thus appear to be partly mythological figures, or, if real, still retain some supernatural overtones from the mythology of the earlier stages of Israelite religion. They are climactic in the series of animals.

The models for the two beasts in nature are the hippopotamus and the crocodile. These two animals are represented here as a contrasting pair; the description of the former emphasizes his vast size and strength as well as his mysterious impassivity and tranquillity, and the description of the latter stresses his fearsome dangerousness. Thus, while the descriptions in the first speech were enthusiastic depictions of nature designed to call attention to God's power and providence, the descriptions in the second speech are occupied more with the character of the animals themselves; unlike the first speech, the second does not make the purpose of the description explicit. The description of the River Coiler, lengthy though it is, breaks off without any marked rhetorical or thematic closure, and the speech itself, the last in Job's thirty-nine chapters of verse, ends without any peroration. The irresistible conclusion is that something is missing.

40:13 *bind them:* literally, "bind their faces." There is some justification in the Bible for taking "face" as a synecdoche for "person."

40:17 *tail:* apparently a euphemism.

40:18 *unyielding:* I find impossibly forced the explanation of most ancient and modern commentators, who, connecting the root of the word here with one of the Hebrew words for a wadi, take it here to mean something tubelike (shaped like a river channel), hence bones. My own solution is based on the fact that in many of its occurrences in the Bible this root means "firm" (as in Job 12:21 and 41:7).

40:19 *Let none but his maker . . . sword:* I.e., only He who made the beast can kill it.

40:23 *gulps:* I admit here to stretching the meaning of the verb, which ordinarily means "to oppress." But the word is sometimes used in connection with stealing, and so it is understood here by some commentators. The idea is that the massive, indolent hippopotamus, when thirsty, simply opens his mouth and lets a vast river slosh into his throat and disappear. Forced as this explanation may seem, it is easier than any possible alternative.

40:24 *thorns:* adopting Ehrlich's emendation of the Hebrew text, which, as it stands, means "with traps."

40:31 *get his head . . . fishnet:* None of the commentaries or translations that I have consulted seems to have recognized that the word here translated as "net" can bear this meaning, and all, therefore, resort to far-fetched explanations or emendations. I have based the translation on the fact that in its frequent appearances in rabbinic literature, it refers to some kind of woven garment. But the syntax remains a bit problematic; as it stands, the sentence means, "Do you fill his head with a fishnet?" instead of "Do you fill the fishnet with his head?" the literal translation underlying my verse version.

41:2–3 *when aroused . . . his presence . . . address him unscathed:* The third person in these phrases is the result of emendations.

41:3 *that man would be mine!:* This sarcastic hypothetical assertion by Yahweh recalls His earlier taunt to the effect that if Job could perform certain feats, even Yahweh would yield to him.

41:25 *dusty earth:* The word "dusty" is used to enforce the comparison with the water, the natural habitat of the River Coiler. Nothing on dry land is as fearsome as this greatest of aquatic creatures.

From its low, flat position in the water, the River Coiler gazes up at dry land's haughtiest creatures, confident of his own superiority. Perhaps Yahweh has chosen this final image in order to leave Job with the thought of his own position relative to the cosmos. Man, too, from his humble place in the dust, imagines himself to be the equal of the loftiest creatures; he thinks that his mind gives him the wisdom to understand and interpret the management of the universe. And like the River Coiler, man does have some real power—in his case, the power of the mind, the sheer energy of the human intellect praised in the first half of the Meditation on

Wisdom. But if man thinks he has any ultimate control or true grasp of reality, he is as deluded as the River Coiler.

42:3–4 *"Who dares . . . Listen now . . . inform me . . ."*: Job quotes Yahweh's words from the beginning of His first speech and comments on them ruefully with his own brief verses.

42:5 *but only by rumor:* Hearing is considered an inferior form of knowing, rhetorically equivalent to not knowing at all; cf. 28:22.

42:6 *I retract. I even take comfort for dust and ashes:* Job's final words are, like so much else in the book, suggestive rather than transparent. I understand the passages as follows: Yahweh's speeches have finally made Job grasp the sheer puniness of man in the scale of the universe and of God. As a result, he realizes the futility of the rage he had so eloquently expressed throughout the book. The resignation he has thus achieved will from now on enable him to endure the loss of all that is merely human: his family, his health, and, in prospect, his own life. But other readers have construed these verses as does the Authorized Version, which reads: "I abhor *myself*, and repent *in* dust and ashes." I do not sense this degree of abjectness in the Hebrew word here translated as "retract"; the dictionary meaning is "reject," and the text does not stipulate the verb's direct object. It seems that the most natural implied object is the totality of everything that Job has said. I do not see how "dust and ashes," the classic Hebrew idiom expressing mortality, can possibly refer literally to dirt and spent coals.

Job's Restoration

42:8 *my servant Job:* Note the fourfold repetition of this phrase.
42:11 *mourned with him and comforted him:* the same words used to describe the intention of the three friends in 2:11.

    qesita: a coin of unknown value, mentioned a few times in the Bible.
42:14 *Horn-of-Kohl:* Kohl, a cosmetic made of antimony, is still in use in the Middle East to make women's eyes appear larger; "horn" refers to an animal horn used as a receptacle for the

powder. Like Dove and Cinnamon, Horn-of-Kohl is thus a name
that suggests feminine beauty. According to a Jewish tradition,
Horn-of-Kohl is the name of a plant, a kind of narcissus.

42:15 inheritance alongside their brothers: mentioned because
it was most unusual for daughters to inherit.

Bibliography

Medieval Commentaries and Standard Translations Consulted

Abraham Ibn Ezra (1089–1164). Jewish polymath from Spain and poet of the Hebrew Golden Age. His commentary on Job was written in Rome c. 1141 and is included in the Rabbinic Bible, the edition of the Hebrew Bible with a selection of Hebrew commentaries published by Daniel Bomberg in Venice, 1524–25. The Rabbinic Bible has been constantly reissued, with new commentaries being added by successive publishers over the centuries.

AV. The Authorized Version of the Bible in English, commonly known as the King James Bible, first published in 1611.

JPS. Translation of the Bible into English by a committee of Jewish scholars sponsored by the Jewish Publication Society (1962–82), replacing its earliest translation of 1917.

Levi ben Gerson (1288–1344). Provençal Jewish philosopher. His commentary on Job, written in 1325, was one of the first Hebrew books to be printed (Ferrara, 1477) and is included in the Rabbinic Bible.

NEB. The New English Bible, an English translation sponsored by a consortium of Protestant church organizations in Great Britain and Ireland and published by Oxford University Press and Cambridge University Press in 1970.

Rashi (Solomon ben Isaac, 1040–1105). Rabbinic authority from Troyes (France) and author of commentaries in Hebrew on most of the Bible. His commentary on Job is printed in the Rabbinic Bible.

Saadiah ben Joseph (892–942). Rabbinic authority in Iraq who translated most of the Bible into Arabic and wrote commentaries in Arabic on many of its books. His translation and commentary on Job was published by J. and H. Derembourg (Paris, 1899); it has also appeared in an English translation by Lenn E. Goodman under the title *The Book of Theodicy* (New Haven: Yale University Press, 1988).

Targum. The translation of Job in Aramaic found in the Rabbinic Bible, thought to have been written in Palestine in the fifth century A.D. or earlier.

Modern Studies and Commentaries

Alonso Schökel, L., and J. Sicre Diaz. *Job: Comentario teológico y literario.* Madrid: Ediciones Christiandad, 1983.

Alter, Robert. *The Art of Biblical Poetry.* New York: Basic Books, 1985.

Bloom, Harold. *Modern Critical Interpretations: The Book of Job.* New York: Chelsea House Publishers, 1988. (Contains essays by Harold Bloom, Paul Ricoeur, Northrop Frye, David Daiches, Robert Alter, and others.)

Butterick, Crim, and Keith George. *The Interpreter's Dictionary of the Bible.* Nashville, Tenn.: Abingdon Press, 1981.

Dhorme, Edouard. *A Commentary on the Book of Job.* Translated by Harold Knight. Nashville, Tenn.: Thomas Nelson, 1984.

Geller, Stephen A. *Sacred Enigmas: Literary Religion in the Hebrew Bible.* London and New York: Routledge, 1996.

Greenberg, Moshe. "Job," in *The Literary Guide to the Bible,* edited by R. Alter and F. Kermode, pp. 285–303. Cambridge, Mass.: Harvard University Press, 1987.

Hakham, Amos. *The Book of Job* (in Hebrew). Jerusalem: Rav Kook Institute, 1984.

Hoffman, Yair. *Blemished Perfection: The Book of Job in Its Context* (in Hebrew). Jerusalem: Bialik Institute, 1995.

Mitchell, Stephen. *The Book of Job.* Rev. ed. San Francisco: North Point Press, 1987.

Pope, Marvin H. *The Anchor Bible: Job.* Garden City, N.Y.: Doubleday, 1965.

Sanders, Paul S. *Twentieth-Century Interpretations of the Book of Job.* Englewood Cliffs, N.J.: Prentice Hall, 1968. (Contains essays

BIBLIOGRAPHY

by Gilbert Murray, Edward Kissane, Arnold Toynbee, and Kenneth Rexroth, among others.)

Terrien, Samuel. *The Iconography of Job Through the Centuries.* University Park, Pa.: Pennsylvania State University Press, 1996.

Index